GLOBAL BUSINESS SERIES

Doing Business with Taiwan

Doing Business with Korea

Doing Business with Singapore

Doing Business with Thailand

Doing Business with China

Doing Business with Mexico

Doing Business
with Taiwan

Paul Leppert

jain
PUBLISHING
JAIN PUBLISHING COMPANY
Fremont, California

This book is designed to provide helpful information for people doing business in Taiwan. It is sold with the understanding that it is not meant to render legal, accounting, medical, or other professional advice. For such services contact a competent practitioner. Some are listed in this book.

Library of Congress Cataloging-in-Publication Data

Leppert, Paul A.
    [Doing business with the Chinese]
    Doing business with Taiwan / Paul Leppert.
        p.   cm. -- (Global business series)
    Originally published: Doing business with the Chinese.
Sebastopol, Calif.: Patton Pacific Press, ©1990, in series: Asian
business series.
    Includes index.
    ISBN 0-87573-041-8
    1. United States--Commerce--Taiwan. 2. Taiwan--Commerce--United
States. 3. Taiwan--Economic conditions--1975- 4. National
characteristics, Chinese. 5. Business etiquette--Taiwan.
    I. Title.   II. Series
HF3130.L44   1995
650'.0951--dc20   95-14753
                                                              CIP

Contents

Introduction

Although it is the size of Maine and has fewer people than California, Taiwan is the thirteenth largest world trading nation and the fourth largest exporter to the United States. Taiwan's foreign exchange reserves, over ninety-two billion dollars, are exceeded only by Japan's.

There is immense potential for business profits in Taiwan. The government there encourages foreign trade and investment. Chinese capital is available and there is an ample supply of trained, low-cost workers.

If you are an American businessman who is planning to visit, live, or do business in Taiwan, you will find that an understanding of local cultural and business practices is essential.

There are many tourist guides to Taiwan and the Government of the Republic of China will send you information on investment laws upon request.

Yet there is a lack of information available to help American businessmen face the practical problems of operating in Taiwan's unfamiliar environment. Most business publications do not address the social, cultural, and political impediments related to doing business with Taiwan.

The first part of this handbook deals with the problems of understanding your Chinese counterpart. He is also a businessman, but due to the influence of his culture, his thought process and ways of doing business are much different than yours. It is worth taking some time to examine the structure of his family, society, culture, work ethics, politics, and law. All of these have a bearing upon the ways Chinese do business.

The second section of this handbook deals with the economic and business environment in Taiwan. You will want to understand current business and economic conditions and how they came to exist. If your business is just beginning to consider Taiwan, the chapter on how to get help in doing business there will be beneficial. Information is also included on how American and Chinese businessmen view each other, procedures for Chinese etiquette, and techniques for business bargaining and negotiation.

The final section of this handbook is concerned with your personal experience of Taiwan; travel tips; things to do, see and learn; addresses of contacts; and a list of additional reading.

I visited Taiwan and talked with dozens of government officials and businessmen. I also interviewed members of the American business community. I have observed conditions in Taiwan since 1958. Never has rapid social and economic change been more evident. Taiwan today is a mixture of old and new. Your Chinese business counterpart will vary in his cultural orientation and business practices depending upon his degree of westernization, position in society, and the specific province from which his family originated.

This handbook is designed to be used as a quick primer and a ready reference. It will provide you with a broad and basic knowledge of Taiwan and enable you to speak and act as an informed person as you enter this new and exciting business arena. It is not designed to give advice for specific business situations and does not represent the positions of the United States government or the government of Taiwan, Republic of China. Conditions are constantly changing. It is best to check the agencies listed here for the most current information.

PART ONE

Knowing Your Counterpart

Knowledge is power. Before you begin your business dealings with Chinese you will want to learn everything you can about them as individuals. How do these people view themselves, their families, society, culture, work, and politics? Chinese attitudes toward these institutions and relationships have a profound impact upon the way they do business. Only by understanding your Chinese counterpart as an individual can you begin to understand him as a businessman.

When two people from different cultures do business, each responds to the relationship according to his own psychological conditioning. People in all cultures are socially conditioned as children. By the time they reach adulthood, cultural assumptions are etched in their minds as indelibly as the circuits of a computer chip. Psychosocial imprinting is mostly subconscious and it is almost impossible to escape its dictatorial controls.

If you understand your Chinese counterpart's thought and behavioral patterns and he does not understand yours, you will go into a business negotiation with a great advantage. You will, to a large extent, be able to predict his attitudes and behavior. But you should not assume that he will be ignorant of your cultural conditioning. Chinese have been studying and manipulating westerners for a long time. Many Chinese have access to our ways of thought because they speak English. In contrast, few Americans speak a Chinese dialect.

1. Childhood and Family

The Role of the Family

During my recent visit to Taiwan my Chinese friends told me of sweeping changes which had "uprooted Chinese society." I then asked them to rank the following in order of importance: self, family, and country. All of them ranked family first, followed by self and country. This response was exactly the same they gave me thirty years ago. In Chinese society, the more things seem to change the more they appear to remain the same.

To understand your Chinese business counterpart you need to understand the prime role of the family. The family is the most important unit in Chinese society and seems to be responsible for almost everything. It provides economic sustenance, controls crime, functions as a nursery and retirement home, furnishes recreation, and encourages feelings of belonging and participation. So much human energy goes into the Chinese family that little is left for society in general.

The primacy of the Chinese family is shown in the fact that, when introduced, Chinese give their family names first. Chinese names usually consist of three characters. The first character is the family name. The second character is usually shared with brothers and cousins of the same generation. The third and last character is the individual's own name which is equivalent to American first names.

Birth

Chinese love children and the birth of a baby is considered to be a great event. It signifies a continuation of the family through the countless generations represented on the ancestral tablets. For Chinese, it is essential that a couple have at least one male child, preferably as many boys as possible. This is necessary because there is no social security retirement and only sons incur the obligation of supporting aging parents. Couples will sometimes produce many daughters in the hope of having a son. Some Chinese friends of mine now have five daughters. If many attempts fail, some couples will adopt a young boy, sometimes a nephew, to carry on the family line.

Early Childhood

Young children are treated with great permissiveness in Chinese society and are included in virtually every aspect of family life. Chinese children are not separated from the family by giving them their own rooms early in childhood. Instead they sleep with their parents and learn to be dependent upon them.

The trauma of toilet training is introduced later than in the West. Some parents will cut a hole in a baby's pants so it can relieve itself at will. Chinese mothers will often nurse their babies on demand, regardless of the social situation. Weaning takes place later than in the West.

Young children are included in virtually every aspect of family life. It is common in Taiwan to see an entire Chinese family, toddlers and all, enjoying a Sunday outing or gathered about a round table while eating in a restaurant. Children seem to be very high on the Chinese social agenda. If you have young children with you, they will be received with open arms. Our young daughter was coddled and spoiled with too much attention. Our

Chinese friends called her "mei-mei," meaning "little sister." Having a young child with us made us a more acceptable social unit and opened many doors.

Early childhood training emphasizes acceptance by the family and a natural, uninhibited upbringing. The child is never made to feel guilty and is seldom rejected. The feeling of dependence which results from this system of child rearing is so strong that Chinese people are subject to considerable parental control for the rest of their lives.

School

When a child enters school, he becomes subject to strict discipline. Corporal punishment is common. The pupil must bow to his teacher and accept authority without question. The days of permissiveness are over.

Parents feel it is important to enroll their children in the best elementary schools. The "right" elementary school leads to the "right" middle school, and eventually, to the "right" university. Graduates of the best universities obtain the best jobs. Parents prepare their children for entrance exams at a very early age. I saw children who were only four or five years old preparing for exams by working through handbooks of problems, much like American students study for the scholastic aptitude tests.

The elementary school curriculum stresses moral, political, and social values which must be accepted on faith. The child reads stories which teach him to value Chinese tradition, authority, and filial piety. If he harbors any desire to rebel he will have a difficult time finding examples. When he goes to the movies, sections of Western films showing unacceptable behavior by Chinese standards are censored. For example, a section of film showing an American daughter slapping her mother will be "cut," resulting in an unexplained jump in the movie's continuity. Such moral censorship eliminates undesirable role models.

Most lifetime friendships will originate in school. Such friendships are more meaningful and deeper than those which will develop later in life. A business friendship between an American and a Chinese will have to be nurtured for many years to even approach the intensity of a school friendship.

The Chinese language has no alphabet. There are thousands of characters and each must be learned by rote. Sheer memory is needed. Each character must be written using the proper order of strokes. Some characters have thirty or more strokes. Chinese students use the same approach to their study of English; they memorize their lessons, word for word, chapter by chapter. If they later attend an American university they will quickly memorize facts. But many Western educators agree that Chinese often have trouble mustering the analytical skills so necessary in American graduate work. The practice of questioning prevailing wisdom is not taught in the Chinese educational system.

Chinese education is characterized by conformity. Elementary and middle school students wear uniforms and chant their lessons together. Individual expression is subordinated to the standards of the group. The norm is to blend in and never stand out. Many Chinese hesitate to express a contrary opinion until they are middle-aged. This system of education produces young adults who are compliant, polite, and somewhat boring. By western standards, individual personalities, at least in public, hardly exist and will not emerge until the age of thirty-five or forty.

The System of Education in Taiwan

Public education in Taiwan is free and compulsory through the ninth grade. Over ninety-five percent of all workers have completed the ninth grade. The government is paying special attention to vocational training and all employers are required to contribute funds for this purpose. Literacy is almost universal. There are 101 colleges and universities on Taiwan. The supply of intelligent workers who are trained in engineering and technical skills is not adequate. So Taiwanese semiconductor engineers, one-fifth of California's silicon valley scientists, are returning to Taiwan to take advantage of good job offers, expanding supplies of venture capital, and growing political freedoms.

Higher Education

The turning point of a person's life often hinges upon whether or not he is accepted for enrollment in a university. College entrance is based upon examination and the competition is ferocious. Huge numbers of young people compete for very few openings. Disciplines, such as engineering and medicine, which provide graduates with the most income and prestige require the highest exam scores for matriculation. Young people who fail entrance exams have been known to commit suicide.

Marriage

For those attending college, it is expected that marriage will wait until graduation. Parents no longer arrange the selection of mates but many exert some influence. Dowries are still customary. Rich men seek to marry their daughters to physicians or government officials. Marriage is forbidden to anyone with the same family name even though no blood relationship exists.

The bride will usually move in with the husband's family and assume a subordinate position to her mother-in-law.

Middle-Age

The Golden Age for a woman begins when her son marries and brings a daughter-in-law into the household. Now the mother's personality will become more assertive. Although she will work hard and defer to her husband in public, she may abuse him in private. Some explosive Chinese wives are called "tea kettles" because they rest an arm on a hip, like a handle, while venting their steam. High ranking Chinese military officers I met while serving as a naval attache told me of their special club, the *Pa Tai Tai Ji Le Bu,* "Afraid-of-Wife-Club." Everyone seemed to be a member.

Some young couples seek to avoid the tyranny of a mother-in-law by moving to a small apartment. When they do this they may incur considerable family disapproval.

Family Obligations

Chinese are usually shocked to find that a westerner will "do his own thing" without regard for his family. This sense of individualism seems alien to Chinese who feel that family obligations should come first.

When we forget the dominance of the family we are likely to misinterpret the behavior of Chinese. I have seen many auto and motorcycle accidents in Taiwan. Few Chinese endangered themselves by trying to help the victim. This reluctance is almost universal and is a matter of family obligation rather than cowardice. If a Chinese successfully rescued the victim he might be obligated by tradition to support him. If he died while trying to help, his action would bring sorrow to this family. So most people in Taiwan will pretend not to see a person who has been injured in an accident.

Family obligations are used as a means of social control. To violate the code of society will bring discredit upon one's family. Asian societies use this sense of shame in place of the sense of guilt used as a means of control in the West. But as Taiwanese society becomes more modern and mobile, social controls are disintegrating.

Old Age

When you become old, Taiwan is a good place to be. Old people are treated with respect and maintain their importance in the family. They are not shunted aside as they are in the West. Old age even begins later in life. At the age of sixty a person may still be considered too young to become a top social, political, or business leader. Most of these are in their seventies or eighties.

The Chinese practice that westerners call "ancestor worship" is not really worship but a memorial veneration of one's ancestors. One reason that old people are honored in China is because they will soon become ancestors.

Long life is symbolized in many ways: the longest possible noodles, peaches, scrolls with one hundred long-life characters, and even turtles!

Importance of the Clan

The clan traces its ancestry back through male family members to a common person. Usually this record is traced as far as the first clan member to enter the area. Taiwanese, for example, usually do not record their ancestry back to mainland China although that is where most Taiwanese families originated. Some clans have thousands of members. Clans are involved in births, marriages, education, charities, and funerals. While the role of the clan has diminished in urban areas it is still important in the countryside.

2. Society

The Question of Change

During my recent visit to Taipei it was obvious that there were great changes. A modern city was rising from the conglomeration of villages which once formed the town. The pace of new construction was rampant and the pace of life was hectic. Skyscrapers were rising from paddy land and gardens. I remarked to a taxi driver that "Taipei is growing." He answered by saying that "Taipei is disturbed."

The attitudes toward social change seem to be many and diverse. Many Chinese businessmen told me that the old traditions were gone, buried in an avalanche of modern materialism. Others insisted that the pace of change was slow and the old traditions still had a solid hold on society.

The old parts of Taipei still have open drainage ditches and hordes of street vendors hawking Chinese viands. On Nan King East Road the entrance to the showroom of the Cadillac dealership is blocked by hundreds of parked motorcycles.

Many questions remain to be answered. How much has Chinese society really changed? Is technology a veneer which covers a traditional Asian social system or has it produced radical social change? Do Taiwanese businessmen operate from the perspective of traditional social values or do they function within the context of modern business practices? What are the attitudes and responses of this most traditional of human societies toward the revolutionary impact of modern industry and technology?

Confucius

To understand the current state of Chinese society and its ramifications for business we have to start with Confucius. Confucius was not the only influence upon Chinese society but he is probably a more powerful figure to the Chinese than Jesus is to westerners.

The great teacher was born in 551 B.C. in the province of Shantung. He died in 479 B.C. Confucius did not create his ethical code but systematized and promoted one that already existed. His social teachings are concerned with human relationships and involve unequal obligations. His system primarily involves the family: the obedience of the son to the father, of wife to husband, of younger brother to older brother. He also established ideal relationships involving duties of friend to friend and subject to ruler. The nation and society were considered to be extensions of the family.

Confucius taught that failure to fulfill these obligations would upset the natural order of things. The ruler had to perform the rites to heaven exactly as prescribed. If times were troubled, perhaps by famine, flood, or war, it was due to the failure of the ruler to perform the rites properly. The emperor therefore lost the mandate of heaven and it was appropriate to overthrow him.

While this system of carefully structured human relationships has been largely maintained in Taiwanese family life, Confucian concepts have been difficult to apply to the problems of technology. Confucius had nothing to say about traffic laws or behavior when boarding a bus. Consequently, in Taiwan these activities tend to border on bedlam. People will form a queue at a bus stop and then dissolve into a mob when the bus arrives. The sage was also silent on the matter of business contracts. Some Chinese businessmen still feel that a handshake is sufficient; a person's honor should be enough to guarantee his conformance to a verbal agreement.

Family Versus Society

The Confucian ideal promotes an hierarchical, status-conscious structure for society. Obedience, filial piety, and respect are heavily stressed. All relationships are unequal. In emphasizing the family, Confucius minimized the importance of society as a whole. For this reason it is difficult for Chinese to muster the type of community spirit and nationalistic fervor so often seen in the West.

Sun Yat-sen, the father of modern China, once said that the Chinese were like many grains of sand, each grain a family, with no cement to hold them together. Chinese place their families above all else. They give much to their families and are little concerned with the rest of society.

The Japanese have a greater sense of community, society, and nationalism than the Chinese. Since Japan ruled Taiwan for fifty years, some of these values were instilled in the island's residents.

But, by Western standards, there is still little sense of community. In the years I lived in Taiwan I often saw housewives and servants sweep the dust from courtyards to the edge of the street. There were always little piles of dirt outside the gates. From the windows of the express train rolling through the verdant countryside one can still see villages with piles of trash next to apartments; people throw their garbage out their windows.

Status Versus Achievement

In the West the individual is usually held responsible for his station in life. Whether or not he achieves prestige, power, and wealth is considered to be the result of his own character, drive, and ambition. Most Western nations are achievement-oriented societies.

In contrast traditional China produced a society which was static and status conscious. Under the old system one did not feel the burdensome responsibility to become something else. One could feel contented within oneself. This is rapidly changing and today Chinese are less likely to accept the place in life into which they were born.

Many of the innovative achievements of the West have been due to the basic restlessness of Western Man, who often has an uneasy feeling that he ought to be doing more. Today many Chinese also feel this sense of restlessness. They have given up acceptance in favor of individual initiative and assertiveness. This manifests itself in the Taiwanese conduct of business and represents a major change in the nature of Chinese society.

Poverty

Poverty is most often ignored by the average Chinese and is assumed to be due to laziness. One takes care of his own family and relatives; that is enough. Living standards have steadily improved in Taiwan but some poverty remains. Except for the activities of clans and some churches, there is little in the way of charitable concern.

"Face"

Face is an Asian word for the concept of dignity. To "lose face" is to experience tragedy and humiliation. In your business dealings it is important never to give offense. Be courteous to your Chinese counterpart and be modest about yourself.

Chinese use many subtle devices to make another person feel good. They use the word "mansion" when referring to another person's house. When referring to their own homes, they use the word "hovel." Chinese dealing with officers of the U.S. Military Advisory Group routinely addressed them by one rank above their actual ranks. I was a major and they addressed me as "lieutenant colonel." Such Chinese practices leave the other person with a good feeling. Try to do the same for them.

Coordination

Chinese realize that they have problems with coordination and communication. They have an old adage: 'When one Chinese fights one Japanese, the Chinese will win. When two Chinese fight one Japanese, the Chinese will lose." "Confused as a Chinese fire drill" is an accurate description. Chinese find it difficult to work together in a coordinated fashion in ways which are assumed in the West. An American businessman with a Chinese staff must give extra emphasis to coordination and communication in order to develop an effective organization.

Violence and Crime

There is very little violence and major crime in Taiwan. Face to face crime in Taiwan, such as murder, assault, and robbery rarely occurs. The streets are safe to walk at night. For a Chinese to show his face as a criminal is to lose face. With increasing westernization, this is changing. There have been a few armed bank robberies in recent years. Theft has always occurred and is rampant in some areas.

Privacy

Chinese do not follow Western concepts of privacy.

Westerners on Taiwan often complain that their amahs barge into any room at any time, without knocking. Men can sometimes be seen urinating in streets and alleys in public view. It is considered acceptable to stare at strangers. Chinese will often ask you what you paid for your possessions since they need to know the value of things for bargaining purposes.

Toward a World Society?

For forty centuries Chinese society was so strong and stable that it easily absorbed all others which entered its sphere of influence. Now it is being transformed by the multiple influences of urbanization, industrialization, technology, and westernization.

Urbanization is breaking up extended families. People move to the cities to take jobs in factories. They can only afford to rent small apartments. Many family members are left on the farm. Women become wage earners and family decision makers. They no longer have the time to make daily visits to outdoor markets for leisurely bargaining and village gossip. Instead, food is hurriedly purchased and stored in refrigerators.

The Chinese have always been materialistic, but never at the expense of their culture. But now the hold of tradition is weakening. There is something in Western style technology which tears at the fabric of traditional societies. The compulsive pace of life, the anonymity provided by cities, and the brutality of cost-efficiency take their tolls. The old tradition extolled good human relationships and asked people to love others and use things. The values of the new society too often compel people to love things and use others. The new economic order improves living standards but produces social instability.

Because Taiwan has been politically separated from mainland China, it has been forced to rely upon Japan and the United States as social and cultural models. Western influence has brought McDonald's, Kentucky Fried Chicken, American style coffee shops, Little League, discos, and automatic vending machines to the island.

Many sociologists feel that all modernizing nations must become members of a new world society. No country can cling to an old social system because it takes both hands to grasp the new. Yet many people in Taiwan feel torn between the proven values of the past and the rapidly unfolding but unknown future of modern technology. Because they are such conservative people, many Chinese think their society is changing faster than it really is. This perception greatly magnifies their pain and anxiety.

3. Culture

Business and Culture

An article in a Hollywood newspaper recently stated that Pepsi had to cancel its "Come Alive with the Pepsi Generation" billboard campaign in Taiwan because this slogan translated into Chinese as "Pepsi Will Bring Your Ancestors Back from the Dead." An American entertainer in Taipei advertised her appearances in Chinese by stating that her performances "would suffocate you" when she meant to say they "would leave you breathless." Obviously, an understanding of Chinese culture and language is essential if you are to do business effectively in Taiwan.

Your Chinese business acquaintance sees the world differently from you. His cultural assumptions guide his behavior and you need to understand these to understand him.

Chinese are not inscrutable. They follow the rules of their culture even more than Americans follow theirs. Learn their culture and you will understand them. But it is best not to make value judgments. One culture can not be judged using the standards of another. Each is an entity.

Chinese businessmen are favorably impressed by Americans who show that they have taken the trouble to learn something about Chinese culture. The American business representative in Taiwan needs to know more than basic etiquette. To gain the respect of his Chinese associates he should know something about Chinese festivals, painting, calligraphy, literature, religion, music, theater, handicrafts, cuisine, and language.

Culture and History

A society is held together by its culture. Culture, in turn, is derived from history. Each person's psychological makeup is based upon subconscious assumptions patterned by the past. We carry this historical baggage lightly because we seldom realize it is there.

Western man is the product of many revolutions: the Renaissance, the Reformation, the Enlightenment, and the many other industrial, political, and social revolutions which crowd Western history. We feel familiar with change. The Chinese, in contrast, have always valued stability and continuity. For thousands of years China viewed itself as the only high civilization in the world. The characters for China translate as "Central Kingdom." China was indeed surrounded by barbarians. The lack of stimulation from other cultures kept China in an isolation that nurtured both stability and splendor. One by one, dynasties took power, ruled, and crumbled into the dust of history. Through all the centuries the Chinese stubbornly maintained their ancient culture. In the process they became the world's most conservative people.

Chinese do not lack inventiveness. They produced the first compass, printing, and gunpowder. But they made little use of these because they were afraid of change. Tradition decreed that man must honor nature and live within it. The natural order must not be disturbed. In contrast Western history is replete with brash efforts to conquer nature and manipulate the natural order of things. This profound difference in cultural attitudes toward nature had great consequences for both societies. China never considered change until faced with overwhelming Western military and industrial technology in the last century.

Festivals and Holidays

American businessmen seeking low cost Chinese labor in Taiwan are often surprised to find that there are seventeen legal festivals and holidays during the year. Many of these involve a break from work for several days. Some holidays are based on the Western calendar. Others follow the Chinese lunar calendar.

Holidays celebrated on dates determined by the Western calendar include the anniversary of the founding of the Republic of China on the first of January, the birthday of Confucius on September 28th, and the Double Tenth National Day which celebrates the 1911 revolution against the Ching Dynasty on October 10th.

Many festivals are held on dates determined by the Chinese lunar calendar which has been in effect for nearly five thousand years. Lunar New Year's Day is held on the first day of the first moon. This is usually in late January or early February. Everything closes down for a week or two. Food must be purchased and stored in advance since stores will be closed. Chinese clean their houses, pay their debts, present bonuses to servants, and visit friends and relatives. Children are given bright red envelopes stuffed with money. People living in the cities return to their villages. Trains and buses carry crowds across the island.

The Lantern Festival, held the fifteenth day of the first moon, proclaims the end of the New Year's holiday season. Lantern competitions are held at major temples with feasts and fireworks. The brightest lantern is said to be the one which "sees the most ghosts."

Two festivals celebrate the birthdays of goddesses. Kuan Yin, Goddess of Mercy, is honored on the nineteenth day of the second moon. Matsu, Goddess of the Sea, is revered on the twenty-third day of the third moon. The most colorful celebrations of her birthday are held at Peikang in central Taiwan and at Tainan in the south.

On the fifth day of the fifth moon the Dragon Boat Festival brightens the spring with flotillas of long, narrow, crowded boats. In ancient times at least one boat was capsized. The crew, in drowning, offered their lives to the gods of fertility. This holiday also commemorates the suicide by drowning of a virtuous poet and minister of state, Chu Yuen.

The fall is considered to be the best time to look at the moon. The Moon Festival is held on the fifteenth day of the eighth lunar month. Yangminshan, Grass Mountain, is a favorite viewing place for people from Taipei. Instead of a man in the moon, the Chinese folk tale tells of a rabbit and a beautiful woman.

During all of these holidays and festivals hotel accommodations are tight and public transportation is very crowded.

Painting

Chinese traditional painting says much about the relative importance of the individual and nature. In a landscape of soaring mountains a human figure is nearly as small as a dot. Big nature, small man. The standard for Chinese landscape painting was set by Kuo Hsi, who was born about 1020. In his sensitive renditions of mountains and clouds, he showed that landscape art is really a state of mind.

Calligraphy

Calligraphy, brush painting of Chinese characters, is considered to be the highest Chinese art form. Because calligraphy requires some knowledge of Chinese characters, this art is probably the least appreciated by westerners.

The art of calligraphy lies in the ability to form the strokes and characters in such a way as to create the mood, pattern, or rhythm which will add to the artistic quality. For example, a sad statement may be drawn in such a way that the characters, as well as the message, express sadness. Thus the content of the message and the means of writing it reinforce each other.

Calligraphy is a very ancient art. Chia Ku Wen, or bone inscriptions, were rendered in the earliest days of Chinese history.

Literature

Chinese literature prominently features the Confucian classics. The Five Classics include the *Shih Ching* (Book of Poetry or Odes), the *Shang Chu* (Book of History), the *I Ching* (Book of Changes or Soothsaying), the *Ch'un Ch'iu* (Spring and Autumn Annals), and the *Li Chi* (Book of Rites). The Four Books include the *Lun Yu* (Analects, the primary source of information on Confucius), the *Book of Mencius, Book of Great Learning,* and the *Doctrine of the Mean.*

Much Chinese literature is available in translation. One of the most famous works is *Romance of the Three Kingdoms,* which describes huge rebellions after the Latter Han Dynasty. This tale is the origin of Mao's statement that "To rebel is justified." Other famous books include *Shui Hu Chuan (All Men Are Brothers,* a story about a gang similar to Robin Hood's), *Dream of the Red Chamber,* and *The Monkey.*

China's two greatest lyric poets, Li Po and Tu Fu, lived in the eighth century. They were called "landscape poets" because they extolled nature. Li Po reputedly drowned when he became drunk and leaned too far out of a boat while trying to kiss the moon.

Philosophy

Chinese are very secular people. Confucianism and Taoism are not religions. They are ethical philosophies. Confucius concerned himself only with the problems of this world and refused to speculate about life after death.

The philosophy of Taoism, founded by Lao-tse in the sixth century B.C., stresses meditation and inaction. In Taiwan this philosophy is practiced in a superstitious way which borders on animism. The word *Tao* means "The Way." "The Way" cannot be adequately defined. It is the unseen energy in nature which must be experienced intuitively. One learns "The Way" through parables.

Both Taoism and Confucianism stress concepts of achievement by living in accordance with the rules of nature.

Religion

Chinese are eclectic about religion. If one religion is good, why not believe in all? Many consider themselves to be "part-time" Christians or Buddhists. American missionaries in Taiwan find it very difficult to accept this attitude.

People in Taiwan are very practical about their local gods. Gods who answer prayers are promoted and assigned larger territories; everybody loves a winner. Gods who fail may end up in the garbage dump. There are all varieties of gods: village, kitchen, and home gods; wooden, plastic, and stone gods. They come and go, rise and fall.

Throughout history foreign religions flowed into China. The Chinese were too worldly to be dominated by any religion but some satisfied needs that were not served by Confucianism and Taoism.

Buddhism was imported into China from India. Chinese practice it at birth, old age, death, and times of withdrawal from society. A favorite Buddhist bodhisattva, supernatural representative of the historic Buddha, is known as Kuan Yin, The Goddess of Mercy. She takes a role similar to the Madonna in Christianity. Statues of Kuan Yin often feature her with a lotus flower in her hand. This is a white symbol of purity because it rises bright and clean from mud and slime.

Although Buddhism is the major religion of Taiwan, Islam and Christianity are both widespread. Chinese bearing the family name of "Ma" are likely to be Mohammedans. Christian missionaries have been active in Taiwan for many years.

Chinese Opera

The opera is a combination of circus, ballet, and musical. The stories are based upon classical and romantic tales. The costumes are colorful and symbolism is important. A warrior dismounts by throwing his riding whip on the floor. Flags patterned like waves mean "storm at sea." Facial makeup signifies the character of the actors. A white face indicates a treacherous character. Gods have gold faces, devils, green.

The players are accompanied by traditional Chinese instruments, the two-stringed erhu and the guitar-like pipa. The conductor beats the drum and sets the pace. Male actors sometimes take female parts.

Unlike Western audiences which usually sit quietly at the opera, Chinese display their approval with loud comments to each other. Inept performers are laughed off the stage. Do not ask your Chinese counterpart to translate for you. The opera is sung in a classical Chinese which few Chinese understand.

Music

Traditional Chinese music, as exemplified by the

opera, has little harmony but much rhythm. A modern Taiwanese musician, Hsu Tsang-houei, developed an interesting synthesis of Western and Chinese music.

American music is very popular, especially among young people.

Handicrafts

Handicrafts on Taiwan include creations in lacquer, metal, bronze, wood, bamboo, and cloth. The care which is taken may be illustrated by the handicraft of lacquerware. This process began in the Chou Dynasty in southern China some two thousand years ago. Its original purpose was to preserve furniture from deteriorating in the hot, moist climate. The lacquer itself is made from the sap of the Chinese sumac. The wood is seasoned in the elements for many years. The object, such as a teacup or tray, is carved by hand. Two primer coats, usually of pig's blood and blue clay, are applied. They are allowed to dry and then sanded. After many coats the object receives a final sanding with fine-grain sandpaper and pumice.

Cuisine

Chinese reserve their finest efforts for their cuisine. I have travelled widely and consider Chinese cooking to be the best in the world.

A description of Chinese provincial cooking and an explanation of the rules of table etiquette are contained in Chapter 12. For now it is sufficient to say that many of China's greatest essays were written about famous banquets. If you ever find yourself at a loss for a topic of conversation with your Chinese business counterpart bring up the subject of food.

Language

Since China produced the seminal culture of East Asia, the ability to speak, read, or write the language draws respect anywhere in the area. In Taiwan, Mandarin, the dialect of Peking, is a first or second language for everyone. It is the official language. A basic fluency in spoken Mandarin is not difficult to obtain. There is little grammar so you need not spend time learning verb conjugations or noun declensions. The meaning is based on tonal inflections and word order. Private tutors of Mandarin are inexpensive in Taiwan and some companies make them available for their executives. The audio-lingual system of learning regards language as a habit, rather than knowledge to be acquired through academic study. It is a greatly satisfying experience to be able to conduct a simple conversation in Mandarin with a Chinese who speaks no English.

China has several dozen spoken dialects and they are not mutually intelligible. Fortunately, each character has the same meaning in all dialects. Because the same character is pronounced differently in each dialect, there is no way to develop a phonetic system or alphabet which all will understand. The character alone allows communication among Chinese who speak different dialects. In Taipei you can often see Chinese from different provinces communicating by tracing characters on the palms of their hands or in the dust or mud.

Written Chinese has a mystique about it because the characters sometimes contain pictographs which seem to define a concept better than the symbolism of the character. If the word "cat" in English contained letters with whiskers and a tail we would have a similar feeling. The characters, by fixing language and thought, helped to make Chinese culture possible. They have been in continuous use longer than any other written language.

Chinese, contrary to the assertions of many authorities,

is not truly monosyllabic. One character seldom represents a word. Usually two or more characters are needed. The use of such combinations lends flexibility for modern usage. For example, the character for "electric" is combined with the character for "talk" to create the word, "electric talk," or telephone. The same character for "electric" is combined with the character for "wagon" to create the word "electric car," or streetcar. Similar combinations create "electric paper," telegram; and "electric shadow " movie.

Some linguists feel that the lack of grammar in Chinese is due to the ancient age of the language. The longer a language exists, the less grammar it employs. Almost by magic the lack of distracting grammar seems to make Chinese a clearer representation of reality. At times Chinese is so terse it is almost a shorthand which needs to be expanded by the imagination of the reader or listener.

The need to memorize thousands of characters in order to read or write Chinese emphasizes the importance of rote memory. In classical times knowledge of Chinese language and literature was a requirement to become an official. Only the sons of affluent gentry who had many years to study could pass the Confucian examinations. This had profound implications for class structure and political power.

4. *Work*

Work Attitudes

The Protestant Ethic lives in Taiwan! It would be difficult to find a more industrious and conscientious work force anywhere in the world. Chinese workers are well motivated by a social system which stresses responsibility to the employer. If a worker falls short of expectations he "loses face." Economic motivation is also strong. In the absence of a safety net such as Western style welfare the worker must rely solely upon his labor for his income. A job is often referred to as a "rice bowl."

The siege mentality in Taiwan also provides a powerful incentive to work hard. The Republic of China has limited international diplomatic recognition so it is forced to go it alone The long confrontation with the Chinese communists has helped forge a cohesive and competitive business community on the island.

Since Taiwan has few natural resources it depends upon the intelligence and hard work of its citizens. Here the island's rural antecedents provide a benefit. Industrialization has brought young women from the countryside to the cities for factory employment. These former farm workers now give the same meticulous care to the production of computer chips that they formerly gave to transplanting tender rice seedlings.

Most Chinese work too hard. The incidence of heart attacks and strokes among government administrators and business executives has been increasing so rapidly that

27

the government is now encouraging people to take holidays and vacations and is threatening to reduce their paychecks if they refuse.

Chinese Business:
An Extension of the Village and Family

In the United States a corporation is usually just a business entity seeking a profit, not a community. In comparison the Chinese corporation or partnership represents an extension of the traditional agricultural community.

In Chinese farm villages the houses are grouped closely together and the farmers commute to the fields. The American practice of locating farmhouses in the center of individual parcels would be considered antisocial in Taiwan. Villages often consist of people who are interrelated.

This same sense of community is carried over to the Chinese firm. The Taiwanese corporation is an integral part of its employees' lives. Business people not only eat and work together, they spend many hours socializing with each other after work. The intent of this practice is to improve personal relationships in order to help everyone work together smoothly.

Companies in Taiwan encourage family members to go to work for the same company. Often a son will take his aging father's job as he would on the farm. Senior executives will often "adopt" a junior manager from another department and act as a kind of godfather or ombudsman.

In family corporations a new generation is taking charge. The young Taiwanese managers I met seemed much more open and flexible than their fathers.

The concept of family is extended even to big companies. Tatung Corporation's chairman, T. S. Lin, stressed the virtue of "unity of thought" in 1983 when he shut off electricity for elevators and air conditioning in order to cut costs. Profits rose in spite of falling sales because Lin used his role as a father figure to obtain support from his workers.

Chinese Business: Decision Making

The design of business offices in Taiwan ensures good communication and enhances group spirit. There are few private offices. Usually there is a large room with rows of desks. Each person's business is conducted in full view and hearing of everyone in the room. The boss is located in the same room and is involved in the office routine. Managers, supervisors, and clerks representing functional areas, such as sales and finance, are seated near each other in order to facilitate coordination.

When problems arise they are discussed until there is a consensual decision. Sometimes it takes a long time to arrive at common agreement. When it *is* reached everyone involved will wholeheartedly support the decision.

Policies tend to originate in mid-management and push up to top officers. Everyone shares responsibility for decisions and their implementation. Chinese business is conducted as a group effort. There are no individual heroes or scapegoats. This is quite different from American business practice.

Role of Businessmen

The place of businessmen in traditional Chinese society was at the bottom. Too often they were avaricious and greedy. They bought and sold commodities in order to corner the market. They produced nothing. The Mandarin word for businessman is *mai-mai ren,* meaning buy-sell man. At one time in Chinese history businessmen were required to wear left and right shoes of different colors in order to designate their low status.

In Taiwan today, businessmen are at the forefront of economic progress. A Chinese executive has high status and he works long hours. If he arrives home before late evening his neighbors will think he is slacking off.

There are many small business enterprises in Taiwan. This is due to the fact that Chinese are natural entrepreneurs and prefer to work for themselves rather than seek lifetime employment with a big company. Many independent middlemen will solicit orders and then look for a manufacturer.

The Role of Workers

During my first visit to Taiwan in 1958, I noticed a crew of manual laborers taking a lunch break, without lunch. When I asked why they had no lunch, I was told that the boss was given the money for their food. Once a week he pocketed the money rather than buying lunch for the workers. The laborers quietly accepted this since it was the custom.

Taiwan's labor practices have come a long way since then, but the capacity of the Chinese worker to perform hard labor for small wages has not changed. The hourly labor cost for both wages and benefits for the average electronics production worker in Taiwan is about one-half the wages and benefits for similar workers in the United States.

Labor Policy

The working day is usually eight hours but may be lengthened to ten under certain circumstances. The work week is usually five and a half days. Overtime wages are paid at one and a half times the hourly rate. Tradition requires payment of a bonus of one or two months' wages at the end of the year.

If a firm employs five or more people, it is required to provide basic insurance for accident, sickness, old age, medical care, and death. The employer usually pays eighty percent of the premiums while the employee pays twenty percent. Companies in specified industries which employ forty or more people must provide vocational education. Companies employing over fifty people are required to contribute to a company welfare fund which is administered by an employee welfare committee.

Factory labor retirement benefits are available for people who have worked for a factory a minimum of twenty-five years. At the age of fifty-five only fifteen years are required.

Savings Rate

The Chinese in Taiwan save an astonishingly high percentage of their income. Taiwan's savings rate has been about thirty-five percent in recent years. This is the highest in Asia. I could not believe this figure until I confirmed it with many Chinese friends. This rate is possible because families work together to save and the government has provided substantial rewards for savings through various programs and the control of inflation.

5. Politics and Law

Chinese Concepts of Law and Government

Ever since their unfavorable experience with legalism in the ancient Chin Dynasty the Chinese have preferred controls based on traditional human relationships rather than law. Chinese seem to want as few laws as possible and they are suspicious of governments which are located too far away. How can distant bureaucrats understand a local situation? Chinese prefer that problems be resolved by people who know them best: family, village, and neighborhood. Their commitments are made to other people rather than abstract legislative concepts.

There is no place for the concept of the loyal opposition in Chinese politics. This is true because modern Chinese politics represents a continuation of many Confucian concepts. The leader of the country is considered to be the father of the national family. One who criticizes the father-leader is acting as a disloyal son; such opposition is counter to the ethic of filial piety which is so thoroughly ingrained in the Chinese mind. The American concept of government which requires a minority party in order to create a democratic process is anathema to many Chinese.

The leader, like the ancient Chinese emperors, is considered to have the "Mandate of Heaven." He has the right to rule as long as he rules well and maintains his prestige. Questioning the leader's right or ability to rule is tantamount to an act of treason in both Taiwan and mainland China.

The Question of Equality

In the West it is assumed that "All men are created equal," at least in the eyes of the law. Chinese tradition assumes the opposite. In Chinese history the literate and powerful made the laws but were seldom required to obey them. Literacy in the form of the ability to write Chinese characters often exempted an accused person from common justice. Even today a professor or politician who violates the law in Taiwan will usually be treated more leniently than a common laborer.

Dr. Sun Yat-sen, the Founder of the Republic of China, felt that people were not equal. Those who "do not know and perceive" must be led by those who do. He envisioned a period of tutelage in which the unthinking masses would be governed by wise rulers. This concept of inequality closely followed Confucian tradition.

Dr. Sun's *Three Principles of The People* was inspired by Lincoln's Gettysburg Address: "Government of the people, by the people, and for the people." Sun interpreted this to mean "nationalism, democracy, and people's livelihood." He led a revolution and established a government to accomplish these goals. His system had five branches of government: legislative, executive, judicial, examination, and censorate. All are now operating branches of the Nationalist government of Taiwan. The last two branches were patterned after traditional Confucian government agencies.

Government of the Republic of China on Taiwan

Since its escape from the communist takeover on the China mainland, the government of the Republic of China on Taiwan has considered itself the only legal government of all of China. The mainland refugees ran both the government and Taiwan with an iron fist for many years. When Chiang Kai-shek died in 1975 his son Chiang Ching-kuo, became president by running unopposed and obtaining all but ten of 1,022 votes. In January, 1988, Chiang Ching-kuo died and was replaced by Lee Teng-hui, a Taiwanese.

Taiwan is one of few Asian nations to boast a steady and peaceful progression toward a more democratic system. A rising business class required a law-based government with transparent decision processes. In May 1991 President Lee declared the end of forty-three years of emergency rule required by the Communist Rebellion. But he stopped short of declaring an end to the formal state of war between the Communists and Nationalists (since 1949) or ending the Nationalists' claim to be the sole legal government of China. In December 1994 the Democratic Progressive Party, which favors Taiwan independence from both the Communists and Nationalists, won the election for mayor of Taipei. In August 1993 a group of Nationalist legislators left the party and founded the New Party, dedicated to ending corruption. These were significant changes because only a few decades ago *any* opposition resulted in stiff jail terms or worse. Eventually the Nationalists will be voted out of office. If they leave peacefully Taiwan will pass its final test as a democracy.

The Constitution, adopted in 1946 when the Nationalists ruled the mainland of China, has five branches of government: executive, legislative, judicial, control, and examination. Each is headed by a *yuan* or council. The Examination *Yuan* gives tests to hire and promote government workers. The first three ,*yuan* are similar to the three branches of U.S. government. The control and examination *yuan* are based on Confucian concepts. The Executive *Yuan* is headed by the prime minister, who is appointed by the president. The president is elected by the National Assembly which is elected by popular vote. The National

Assembly primarily elects the president and amends the Constitution. The Legislative *Yuan* passes the laws.

Security Measures

The civil war between Taiwan and the mainland has become a cold war. Martial law, imposed in 1949, was cancelled in 1987. It was replaced by "security measures." Opposition parties are now legal but many restrictions remain.

Censorship is a natural outgrowth of security laws. In Taiwan movies, television, books, magazines, radio, and mail are subject to censorship. In the American movie, *Dr. Zhivago,* scenes depicting a revolt of Russian troops against their officers were cut. Issues of *Time* magazine have been removed from newsstands because they included photographs of Mao Tse-Tung. Shortwave radios must be licensed and modified so they cannot receive communist stations. Ideas or role models which are not approved by the government are denied access to media.

Modern technology seems to work both for and against security law controls. Computers are used to keep track of people who enter or leave Taiwan. They also record foreign registrants at hotels through a requirement to disclose passport numbers at the time of registration. On the other hand copy machines are located almost everywhere on the island so the authorities have lost control of print reproduction.

The Army

Chiang Kai-shek, as the young Commandant of Whompoa Military Academy, built the Nationalist Army in the early days of the Chinese Republic. In his rise to power he played off one warlord against another. After their defeat by the communists and retreat to Taiwan the Nationalists faced a dilemma. The remnants of their army were barely sufficient to maintain control of Taiwan and lacked the strength to defend the island against communist invasion.

More manpower was needed so the Nationalists decided to draft the local Taiwanese men. This was difficult because conscription has always been unpopular in China; Confucius said that good men should not be used for soldiers. The first attempt to draft the native men failed because the Taiwanese were just too expensive. They had been accustomed to daily hot baths during the period of Japanese rule and in other ways required a higher standard of living. The Nationalists did not have the money for bathhouses, wood, coal, rice, and all the other amenities demanded by the Taiwanese and the draft attempt failed. Sometime later a second attempt succeeded and today the Nationalist army is eighty-five percent Taiwanese.

Until recent years few Taiwanese officers were promoted beyond captain. The government wanted no leaders who might deploy army units as part of a Taiwanese revolt. As an assistant naval attache at the U.S. Embassy in Taipei, I once followed the careers of the few Taiwanese officers who had attained the rank of major in the Chinese Marine Corps.

The abundance of cliques and rival personalities in the Nationalist armed forces ensures an important role for the military in politics but diminishes combat effectiveness. The next generation of leaders upon which the island will have to depend includes many poorly educated military men.

Civil Rights

There are striking differences between American and Chinese concepts of criminal law. Even the most uneducated American takes for granted such guarantees as the

presumption of innocence, limitations on search and sei-
zure, and the right against self-incrimination. Chinese law
has less regard for the rights of the individual and more
closely follows the Napoleonic Code.

If a crime is reported the police may swarm into the
neighborhood and arrest a number of local people who
just happen to be in the area. These residents may be
beaten or intimidated until there are several confessions
to the crime. The local magistrate may then convict and
sentence the person who made the 'best" confession and
release the others upon receipt of suitable guarantees.

A person who has completed a criminal sentence and
is to be released from prison must first find a guarantor
for his conduct. Many thousands of convicts who have
completed their terms remain in prison due to their in-
ability to find such guarantors. Sometimes an entire family will be held responsible for the actions of one of its
members. This *bau-jya* or protect-the-group system is a
continuation of traditional Chinese police practices.

To avoid police intervention people in Taiwan will
sometimes "solve"' their own crime problems. For example, a thief, if caught in the act, might be severely beaten
by an angry mob of neighbors.

In some ways Chinese in Taiwan have more freedom
than Americans. Many local laws are lenient and not en-
forced. Street vendors park their carts on sidewalks without the need for permits. Merchants disrupt the air with
loudspeakers and bullhorns as they hawk their wares.
People sleep in public buildings, bus terminals and parks
without police interference. Zoning and building regulations are lax and often circumvented. Vehicular traffic
is chaotic.

Asian legal and political systems should not be evalu-
ated by Western standards. Each system is the natural result of its own unique culture. Each must be judged by its
own values and history.

Return to the Mainland?

Ever since the Nationalist retreat to Taiwan recovery of the mainland from the communists has been an article of faith. All over the island reminders have been placed to stir memories of the mainland and perpetuate the goal of its recovery. Television programs show scenes of the China the Nationalists left behind. Streets in Taipei have been renamed to reflect the geography of China. Kwangchow Street is in the southern part of town. Peiping Street is in the north. Hankow and Changsha Streets are in the center of the city. Other thoroughfares such as Kuang Fu, "Recovery Road," get more to the point.

The Nationalist's right to rule Taiwan is based upon the claim that it is the legal government of all of China and the promise to "return to the mainland" is a necessary credo to support this claim. Yet nearly all the people in Taiwan were born on the island. Only a few people over the age of fifty-five can remember life on the mainland. The large majority has little desire to risk a war to recover a place it has never seen.

The international position of the Republic of China is quite ambiguous. Few nations now recognize the Republic of China on Taiwan. On January 1, 1979, the United States recognized the People's Republic of China. As part of the agreement with Peking the United States agreed that Taiwan was part of China and declared that reunification of Taiwan and the mainland was an internal Chinese matter to be resolved peacefully. Most other nations had already withdrawn recognition of Taipei. These actions, and the expulsion of Nationalist China from the United Nations left the Republic of China in diplomatic isolation. The native Taiwanese majority was not allowed to vote on the question of independence.

Soon after the United States established diplomatic relations with Red China, our Congress passed the Taiwan Relations Act which encouraged American business with the island. Although American military forces were removed from Taiwan some support continues. An American helicopter company is selling modern helicopters to the Chinese armed forces and former American military personnel are training these forces in operating and maintaining the new aircraft. While these helicopters have greater capabilities than the ones they replace they are still considered to be defensive weapons and thus not in violation of the agreement with communist China. In 1993 the U.S. government allowed sales of 150 F-16 jet fighters to Taiwan despite its promise it would not arm Beijing's rival.

Political Prospects for the Future

Political possibilities for the future include Nationalist reunification with communist China, a revolt of the Taiwanese majority against Nationalist rule, and a gradual transition toward a government in which both mainlanders and Taiwanese would share power.

Communist Chinese invasion of Taiwan would be militarily costly and the diplomatic price would probably be prohibitive. Peking would lose real and potential American and Japanese support which it needs as a balance against Russia. The U.S. Navy might prevent such an invasion in order to protect American business interests on the island. American business now owns over three billion dollars in assets in Taiwan.

Because of these factors the People's Republic of China hopes to manage a peaceful reunification with Taiwan. There have been numerous overtures to Taipei from Peking since 1979. Most of these have been sentimental and cultural enticements to the Nationalist leaders to "come home." The mainland government has rebuilt the old Chiang Kai-shek mansion in Xikou after its destruction by the Red Guards. Even the Chiang family shrine has been refurbished to greet Taiwan's leaders. So far there has been no response from Taipei. In May 1990, Taiwan's president announced a willingness for improved relations. Trade between the two Chinas, conducted mostly through Hong Kong, exceeded three billion dollars a year.

The founders of both Chinas worked closely together in the early days of the republic. Nationalist and communist leaders shared in Sun Yat-sen's revolution and the older men on both sides know each other well. Their civil war has aspects of a family feud.

If the communists can convince the Nationalists to unite, they would gain Taiwan's technology and remove the Republic of China as an alternative Chinese government. But there seems to be little motivation for the Nationalists to reunify as long as they can maintain their power in Taiwan. Many Taiwanese are also opposed to reunification because communist control of the island would threaten the business structure which is mostly Taiwanese.

A revolt by the Taiwanese majority, which comprises eighty-five percent of the population, is unlikely under present circumstances. The rebellion of February 28, 1947, took place under considerably more stringent economic circumstances. Since the early 1950s the Nationalist government has handled the economy adeptly and the standard of living has risen sharply. Per capita gross national product, $12,000, is the second highest in Asia. The Chinese have never revolted against a government during periods of prosperity. In addition, the ruling Nationalist Party has broadened itself to include many native Taiwanese.

It is possible that a Taiwanese revolt would occur only if reunification between the People's Republic of China and the Nationalists seemed imminent. Such a preemptive rebellion would have to be immediately successful or it might cause the reunification it meant to prevent. If the Nationalists felt they were on the verge of losing power they might strike a quick deal with Peking.

Many Taiwanese think reunification is inevitable. They view it as a pending disaster and cite Hong Kong as an example of communist recovery of China's ancient lands through a process of intimidation. Perhaps Taiwan will be next. Affluent Chinese on Taiwan are sending their assets and children to the United States. Large quantities of arms are being smuggled by boat into the southern part of the island. Why sneak weapons into a country which already has heavily armed military forces? The Nationalists claim that communists are behind the smuggling. It is more likely that some Taiwanese are arming to protect themselves against communist troops from the mainland as a result of a reunification agreement. The Taiwanese have been slaughtered by troops arriving from the mainland before.

Accommodation between the mainlander dominated government of Taiwan and the native Taiwanese is likely if reunification can be avoided. Indeed, this transition is already under way. The present generation of leaders represents the last to be born on the mainland. Lee Tenghui, Taiwan's powerful president, was born on the island. Within a few years, all of the leaders will be natives of Taiwan regardless of the provincial origin of their families. When this time comes it would be no surprise to see the Republic of China drop its claim to the mainland and seek United Nations membership and diplomatic recognition as a new and independent nation.

PART TWO

Economy and Business

Taiwan has one of the fastest growing economies in the world. This success is due primarily to the island's ability to build export business. We need to learn more about how this is done because the United States has a large chronic trade deficit with Taiwan. In order to operate successfully in Taiwan, you will need an understanding of how the Taiwanese economy developed and how it functions. This section will also help you with some of the practical problems in establishing business relationships on the island. These topics include information on how to get help in doing business in Taiwan, an analysis of how Chinese and American business people view each other, a description of Chinese standards of etiquette, and a discussion of techniques which can be used in business negotiations.

As we look at the Chinese business and economic environment we must keep in mind the cultural and social perspectives covered in Part I. We can only understand what is going on in the Chinese business world if we approach it from the viewpoint of the Chinese themselves. Here again, culture is a dominant influence.

6. A Brief Economic History

Geography

Taiwan, a link in the chain of islands which fringe the coast of China, is situated between southern Japan and the Philippines. The verdant, subtropical island is shaped like a tobacco leaf. In area it is about 240 miles long and 85 miles across, some 14,000 square miles. The east coast has some of the highest sea cliffs in the world. Soaring mountains plunge precipitously to the sea.

Located on the edge of the Pacific's "rim of fire," the island often shudders. An old Taiwanese legend says that the island rests on the back of a sleeping dragon. From time to time he awakes and stretches, causing earthquakes. When he exhales, sulfur fumes rise from volcanic fissures.

Settlement of Taiwan

The earliest settlers of Taiwan were Malay people. No one knows for sure where these aborigines came from. Various experts place their origin to the north, south, and west. When Chinese people later occupied Taiwan, the Malay natives moved inland. Today, tribes such as the Ami occupy themselves by doing traditional dances and fashioning handicrafts for tourists. They live on isolated reservations much like American Indians.

For thousands of years the emperors of China paid

little attention to Taiwan. The Ming Dynasty claimed Taiwan as a tributary but did little to control it. For a while the island was administratively under Fukien Province. For a long time Taiwan was a haven for Chinese and Japanese smugglers, outlaws, and pirates. Fishing was the major legal industry.

The first permanent Chinese settlements were probably in the sixteenth century. An old legend is told to illustrate the civilizing of the aborigines by the Chinese. These tribes were fierce and waged war almost continuously. A basic motivation for violence between tribes was the need to acquire human heads. They believed that the more human heads they buried in the fields at the time of sowing, the better the harvest. A local Chinese, Wu Feng, tried fruitlessly to end this practice among the Tsou tribe. Finally he offered his own head in sacrifice on condition that it be the last such offering. The Tsous took his head but kept their word and the practice was ended.

Western Discovery

About the time that the Chinese were settling Taiwan the island was "discovered" by the Portuguese, who named it "Ilha Formosa," Beautiful Island. The Chinese inhabitants continued to call it Taiwan, "Terraced Bay."

The Portuguese were followed by the Dutch. The Dutch East India Company established bases at Tainan in the south and at Tamsui, near Taipei. Parts of original Dutch buildings may be seen in both places. Dutch rule was harsh; they set stringent taxes on agricultural production.

Koxinga

In the early seventeenth century there were two reasons for Chinese to flee Fukien Province for Taiwan: famine, and the Manchu threat to invade south China. A Chinese sea adventurer, Cheng Chih-lung, transported many of the refugees to Taiwan in his ships. He also encouraged them to grow sugar and rice on Taiwan's virgin land. Cheng was eventually lured to the mainland by the Manchus. There they violated their pledge of safety and executed him for refusing to turn over his fleet to them. Cheng's son, Cheng Cheng-kung, known in the West as Koxinga, led an attack of a thousand war junks on the Dutch in Taiwan. In 1662, with the help of local Chinese, he ended thirty years of Dutch tyranny. Koxinga's agricultural policies laid the basis for today's abundant crops of sugar cane, rice, pineapples, and bananas. Taiwan now harvests so many bananas it is considered a patriotic duty to eat as many as possible.

In 1683 the Manchus finally conquered the island and squeezed the economy in ways that only imperial Chinese bureaucrats could devise. But Koxinga is still memorialized. At Tainan one can view his monument and the Dutch fort which became his palace.

Manchu Period

In the late nineteenth century the Chinese government, in response to French and Japanese incursions on the island, made Taiwan a province. Liu Ming-ch'uan, the first governor of Taiwan, moved the capital from the southern part of the island to a small village in the north which was renamed Taipei.

Liu's goal was to modernize the economy of Taiwan. In 1887 he turned on the first electric light in Taipei. Two years later railroad tracks were laid from Taipei to the port of Keelung. Liu fortified five ports with Krupp guns. He was so successful in modernizing the island that he was recalled to Peking by jealous reactionary bureaucrats.

During the Manchu period immigration to Taiwan

from the mainland continued. Most Taiwanese living on the island today are descended from settlers who arrived in Manchu times.

Japanese Period

In 1894 the Korean peninsula exploded in a war between China and Japan. Japan had already built a modern war machine and defeated China. In the Treaty of Shimonoseki, which ended the war, Japan received Taiwan.

In an attempt to forestall Japanese occupation, Taiwan declared itself an independent republic on May 23, 1895. To no avail. The Japanese overran the island anyway and began an occupation which did not end until 1945.

Japan took much from Taiwan. The island became a source of food and raw materials for Japan's growing population and industry. The name of the capital was changed from Taipei to Taihoku. Japanese became a required language; all older Taiwanese can still speak it today. The Taiwanese, as colonial subjects, were kept in subservient positions.

Japan also gave much to Taiwan. Public order, transportation, agriculture, electrical power, health, and education were markedly improved. The Japanese established the first public schools on the island. Few tourists at Sun-Moon Lake realize they are at a Japanese built hydroelectric development. Rice production was increased to yield three crops per year. Epidemics of bubonic plague, cholera, and malaria were controlled. The Japanese made Taiwan a modern province and left indelible cultural influences: restaurants which serve sushi and tempura, Japanese houses and music, and the tradition of the hot bath.

During World War II Taiwan grew in importance as a food producer for Japan and as a base for military operations. Many of the ships which participated in the attack on Pearl Harbor sortied from Taiwanese ports.

Time of Troubles

Upon the surrender of Japan at the conclusion of World War II the Taiwanese welcomed the return of Chinese rule. But soon they were disillusioned. Some soldiers of the Nationalist army treated Taiwan as a conquered province and expropriated private property belonging to the Taiwanese.

Within two years Nationalist corruption and excesses under Governor Chen Yi led to the February 28, 1947 rebellion in which the Taiwanese briefly controlled the island. Then massive Nationalist reinforcements from the mainland crushed the revolt. Mass executions and imprisonment of Taiwanese rebels on Green Island followed.

As the Nationalists fled the communist onslaught more and more refugees arrived in Taiwan. By 1949 the city streets had become crammed with tin and cardboard shacks. There were no other places for new arrivals to live. Life looked bleak and hopeless for many of the refugees who arrived without food, money, or jobs. The impact of these refugees upon the labor market increased tensions with the local Taiwanese. On December 7, 1949, the Nationalists named Taipei the capital of all of China and announced they would use Taiwan as a base for the reconquest of the mainland.

Era of Prosperity

The economic situation began to improve in 1950 due to the effects of the outbreak of war in Korea and the start of United States military aid to Taiwan. Soon after the beginning of the Korean War President Truman neutralized the Straits of Taiwan by placing the Seventh Fleet in a position to prevent flare-up of fighting between the Nationalists and the communists. The realization by the Nationalists that they were unlikely to recover the mainland soon led them to develop effective economic plans for the improvement of Taiwan's economy.

The Korean War stimulated an economic boom in Taiwan. American fighting forces relied upon the island for millions of dollars in goods and services from truck repair to radio parts. During this period, Tatung, a company specializing in electronics, became a giant corporation.

Due to Red Chinese involvement in the Korean War the United States moved to build Taiwan into an anticommunist bastion in the Pacific. American economic aid began in 1950. Much of it went to develop Taiwan's infrastructure: ports, railroads, roads, and power supply. In 1965, United States economic aid, having accomplished its purpose, was terminated. A total of 1.5 billion dollars had set the stage for an economic miracle. Taiwan became the first American aid recipient to become economically self-sufficient.

Military aid, which eventually totalled 2.5 billion dollars, continued. Some twelve hundred personnel were assigned to the U.S. Military Assistance Advisory Group (MAAG) in 1951. These advisers soon discovered that the Nationalist Army had many problems: too many officers, lack of command coordination between air-ground-sea branches, and political intrigue. With the help of American training and equipment many of these problems were solved and the Nationalist Army became a modern fighting force.

An international organization, the Joint Committee on Rural Reconstruction (JCRR), did much to improve Taiwanese agriculture and living conditions in the countryside.

Land Reform

In 1953, the Nationalist government moved to eliminate the power of the Taiwanese rural gentry. They did this through compulsory land reform which also increased food production. Landlords who owned more than seven acres of paddy land had to sell the excess to the government. The government paid the landlords less than the market value of the land. Thirty percent of the payment to the landlords were made in shares of four public corporations. The other seventy percent was paid in land bonds which paid interest of four percent, less than the market interest rate.

The former tenant farmer was allowed to buy the land from the government at two-and-a-half times the annual yield of the crops and had ten years to pay. As a result of this "Land to the Tiller" program, the new landowners seemed to work harder and produce more. They also had a freer choice of crops since they no longer had to pay land rent in rice. The consequent increase in the production of cash crops such as citrus, mushrooms, and pineapples greatly increased Taiwan's export position.

New Crises

In the 1970s three events led people to believe that Taiwan's prosperity was ending. Nationalist China was expelled from the United Nations, the United States broke diplomatic relations with Taipei in order to recognize communist China, and the Arab oil sheiks vastly inflated their prices.

When the United States severed diplomatic relations with the Republic of China in Taiwan, it did so with only a few hours' notice. The Taiwanese demonstrated because they thought the United States would allow Red China to invade the island. They showed their anger by confronting Americans on the street and jeering, "Are you still here?"

It looked like Taiwan, isolated and energy-poor, would suffer a great economic depression.

But it simply did not happen. The government and people of Taiwan mustered enough confidence to stand alone. The Republic of China managed to maintain commercial relations with more than 150 nations. The island adjusted to higher oil prices by working harder and exporting more products.

Taiwan's per capita GNP has now soared to twelve thousand dollars. The island remains a major trading partner of the United States. The standard of living in Taiwan is the second highest in Asia, next to Japan's. Today there is a steady flow of American businessmen to Taiwan. Pan American Airways and KLM-Royal Dutch Airlines resumed flights to Taiwan in 1983 despite the objections of communist China. There was just too much business to ignore. Soon other airlines followed.

The government of the Republic of China must be given credit for the success of Taiwan's economy. This achievement has been accomplished through adroit planning by one of the few Asian bureaucracies staffed by trained engineers. Many of Taiwan's government planners and business executives are graduates of American universities. Taiwan is one place where the government knows how to make the economy work.-

In overcoming their crises, the people of Taiwan exhibited the unique Chinese vitality which pervades their history. As the dust rises from the busy streets of Taipei each morning, it resurrects a past which is filled with pirates and princes, scoundrels, monks, and commoners. All were animated with great exuberance. There is no other human record like it.

7. A Look at Taiwan's Successful Economy

An Economic Miracle

The first time I visited Taiwan, in 1958, rickshaws and pedicabs were the most common vehicles on the streets. By the mid-1960s motorcycles were everywhere. During my 1989 visit monstrous traffic jams made it obvious that many people had purchased cars. Problems of parking illustrated Taiwan's entrance to the modern era. The boom in consumer goods was evident. Many stores were selling refrigerators, air conditioners, rice-cookers and other household appliances. The firm of Tatung had even produced a microcomputer for the local market.

Since 1960 Taiwan has had one of the world's fastest economic growth rates. Over the past thirty-five years, the real growth rate has averaged about nine percent. Even in periods of world recession, Taiwan's economy has turned in a creditable performance.

This is even more remarkable because Taiwan accomplished all of this without appreciable natural resources. Taiwan has no oil or iron ore, only some low grade coal and a little gold, copper, silver, and sulfur. The island's main resources consist of some natural gas, abundant rainfall, a limited amount of fertile land, and an industrious population. From this modest base, the government and people of Taiwan have developed a flourishing economy based on such industries as clothing, textiles, electronics, food processing, chemicals, and a variety of consumer goods.

Government Projects to Improve the Infrastructure

Government planners recognize how much an economy needs a reliable and efficient infrastructure. Ten major projects were recently completed. These include petro-chemical developments, an integrated steel mill, improvements to Kaohsiung shipyard, and completion of projects for the North-South Freeway, Taoyuan International Airport, Taichung Harbor, and two nuclear power plants. Twelve new projects include improvement of farm mechanization, construction of a four-lane highway between Pingtung and Oluanpi, improvement of farm irrigation and drainage, additional nuclear plants, improvement of Taichung harbor, new housing projects and cultural centers, construction of dikes along the west coast and rivers, three new cross-island highways, broadening of highways in the Kaoping area, linkage of round-the-island rail networks, and additional steel production capacity.

A construction project in Kaohsiung harbor has converted a small island into a mammoth container terminal. Loading of containers flows directly from truck to ship. An underwater tube has been dropped, segment by segment, to the floor of the harbor in order to create a motor vehicle tunnel connecting the island to the mainland. The workers in the tunnel showed me the flexible connections used to join the segments. These are designed to prevent rupture of the tunnel during the frequent earthquakes which occur in the area. People on the island who lost their houses due to construction of the terminal were employed in the work force once the project was completed.

Basic Industries

Until recently the government has owned or dominated all industries considered to have economic or strategic importance. Through this control it kept prices of basic products such as oil and steel low so downstream industries could keep prices of finished goods competitive in world markets. In October, 1988, the government announced that most public corporations would be privatized with shares listed on the Taipei Stock Exchange. Only a few corporations were to remain public (government owned). Among these are the Chinese Petroleum Company, Taiwan Power Company, Taiwan Sugar Company, Taiwan Fertilizer Corporation, and Taiwan Salt Works. As part of this move away from socialism, steel, aluminum, and shipbuilding will be private.

China Steel Corporation is an excellent example of a Taiwan corporation in action. According to Mr. T. K. Liu, chairman, China Steel has been unable to keep up with demand. Exports have been curbed in order to meet domestic needs. The boom is so hot that new equipment is being installed faster than workers can learn to use it. Management has been computerized, cogeneration of electricity is saving energy, and most operations are automated. At a time that the American steel industry is in the doldrums, the business of China Steel is thriving. Sixty-seven percent of the company's coking coal and fifty-nine percent of its iron ore are imported from Australia. Ninety-four percent of the corporation's exports go to other nations in Asia.

Trade and Trading Companies

There are over forty-five thousand trading companies in Taiwan. This number compares to about two thousand in Japan. Taiwan's trading companies are mostly family owned and too small to compete with the giant foreign firms. In order to improve Taiwan's capability for trade, the government initiated a program to create *"Ta Mao I Shang"* (Big Trading Companies), to develop international trade at all levels. *Ta Mao I Shang* combine the efforts of factories, banks, and export-import concerns. This effort has been only partly successful. Taiwan's trading companies still control only about ten percent of the island's trade. Thirty percent is controlled by Taiwan's manufacturing industries and fully half of all international commerce is conducted by Japan's huge trading companies.

Exports

Taiwan's export program is so successful that the conversion of tens of billions of dollars of foreign exchange earnings into New Taiwan dollars has resulted in too much money in circulation. Such an increase in currency could lead to the inflation that the government is trying hard to avoid. The export boom, showing no signs of cresting, will probably push foreign sales to new highs. Only Japan has larger foreign reserves.

A third of the Republic of China's exports go to the United States. Exports account for about half of the island's gross national product and include such products as textiles, plastic goods, electronics, footwear, machinery, electrical appliances, and agricultural commodities.

Taiwan has a continuing trade surplus with the United States, its most important export customer. The government realizes that too large a surplus could increase demands for protectionism in the United States. When this surplus grew sharply in 1982, the government sent a "Buy American" delegation to the United States to purchase six hundred million dollars in American industrial and farm products. Such delegations have been sent to the United States about twice a year.

Export industries in Taiwan are acutely conscious of

quality control. Only the best products are allowed to leave the island; "seconds" are sold on the domestic market. It is difficult, for example, to find a first-rate orange on a local fruit stand; the best are exported.

The government actively encourages joint manufacturing and export ventures. Toyota, Japan's largest automaker, and the China Steel Corporation agreed in 1989 to join with several Taiwanese companies to manufacture Toyotas on the island. Some 300,000 cars are produced per year. Fully half of all this production is exported.

Imports

Taiwan has a protectionist policy regarding imports. By doing this the government guarantees that Chinese industries will have sufficient unit sales to lower the unit costs of export products. There are high customs duties on foreign products. The government monopolizes the import of alcoholic beverages and tobacco products.

Taiwan imports mainly from Japan (27%), the United States (24%), and the Middle East (19%). Major imports include petroleum, agricultural commodities, chemicals, machinery, metals, and transportation equipments. Government goals include the reduction of Japanese imports and the diversification of oil sources. All of Taiwan's oil is imported. Most of it comes from the Mideast.

The United States finds it difficult to compete with Japanese sales to Taiwan because Japan's transportation costs are lower and delivery is faster due to the short distance between Japan and Taiwan.

Transportation

Taiwan has an excellent transportation grid. Major ports are located at Keelung, Kaohsiung, Taichung,

Hualien, and Suao. Airports serve Hualien, Taichung, Tainan, Taitung, Taoyuan, Kaohsiung, Taipei, and Makung. Eighteen thousand kilometers of roads and highways connect all parts of the island. Completion of a six-lane highway between Keelung and Kaohsiung reduced the road time between the two cities to less than six hours.

The rail system consists of two separate trunk lines. One line runs between Keelung and Kaohsiung on the west coast; the other connects Hualien and Taitung on the east coast. Rail time between Keelung and Kaohsiung is about four hours.

Usage of all forms of transportation has increased with the rapid growth of the economy; so the grid is being expanded. Traffic jams in the streets of Taipei are so frequent that the government is building a mass transit system to relieve the situation. Part of this network is underground.

Banking

The Ministry of Finance has primary control of banking policies and systems. The Central Bank of China supervises the banking system and is responsible for foreign exchange, regulation of money and credit, bank examination, and economic research. It also issues national currency and serves as the government fiscal agent. The Bank of Taiwan acts as fiscal agent for the province and the City Bank of Taipei acts as fiscal agent for Taipei municipality.

According to law, commercial banks may handle short and medium term loans and bill discounts; receipts of checking, demand, and time deposits; investments in bonds; processing of domestic and foreign remittances; guarantees, collections, warehousing; acceptances of commercial drafts; issuance of letters of credit, and sales of public bonds, treasury bills, corporate debentures, and stocks.

The Banking Law designated the role of development banks to provide particular industries with medium and long-term credit. Banks involved in this activity include The China Development Corporation, The Farmer's Bank of China, The Bank of Communications, and the Export-Import Bank of China.

Investment and trust companies accept trust funds and engage in investment activities. The government encouraged the development of these companies in order to resolve a chronic shortage of long and medium-term capital to finance heavy industry and projects to improve the island's infrastructure.

Foreign banks are not allowed to establish more than one branch in Taiwan. The government places some restrictions on foreign banks which are not applied to domestic banks. Local currency savings and time deposits are not allowed and various limitations are placed upon currency deposits, issuance of commercial paper, pre-export loans, and total credit lines. A list of foreign banks currently operating in Taiwan is located in the chapter titled "Useful Addresses." The Nationalist government is studying the possibility of allowing offshore banking. To do this it would have to allow the free flow of information across Taiwan's borders. This would weaken security control of communications. It is possible that, in time, Taiwan could become the Asian equivalent of Switzerland. But no definite policies about this have yet been announced.

Bill finance companies satisfy the supply of and demand for short-term funds. They participate in both primary and secondary markets.

Foreign exchange operations are controlled by the Central Bank of China. Most transactions involving foreign exchange require a license or prior permission and must be conducted through authorized foreign exchange banks. The basic unit of exchange is the New Taiwan (NT) dollar which fluctuates in a limited range from the U.S. dollar. The current ratio is about NT $26 = US $1.

Taiwan Stock Exchange

The Taiwan Stock Exchange, located on the top two floors of the City Building in Taipei, was opened in 1962. Mr. K. C. Peng, chief of public relations, graciously showed me the trading floor operation and allowed me to interview him in my rusty Mandarin. Securities traded include stocks, corporate bonds, and public bonds. More than a hundred companies, mostly manufacturers, are listed. Many are in the textile industry. The trading floor was busy and noisy. Transactions were once calculated with the help of abacuses but now the system is computerized. On nearby floors the offices of brokerage firms were crowded with excited housewives. Mr. Peng explained that Chinese like to gamble and the stock exchange is the only legal place in Taiwan to do so. In order to preclude excessive speculation, daily price changes are limited to five percent. Fu Hwa Securities Finance Company, Ltd., loans money for margin trading. Stock market information and financial data are printed and posted on a wall in a nearby alley to help investors investigate before investing.

The Taipei Stock Exchange has the world's largest volume because the Taiwanese are ardent gamblers. More shares trade daily than on the New York Stock Exchange. The average holding period is only four days. Speculation is so rampant that teachers and workers listen to stock reports on earphone radios and office managers pay brokerage houses to round up their workers. The market is dominated by small investors who do not take losses lightly. When the market lost half its value in the first three months of 1990, they beat up government officials and marched on the finance ministry.

Markets are thin and there is much price manipulation. Taiwan's Securities and Exchange Commission is doing much to resolve these problems. The Taiwan Stock Exchange is not open to nonresident foreigners. The only way for foreigners to participate in the astounding growth of the economy is through a number of mutual funds listed on major world stock exchanges.

Trade with Mainland China

In spite of the animosity between the governments of Taiwan and mainland China, much Taiwanese investment has flowed from Taiwan to the mainland. An estimated five thousand Taiwanese companies have established factories in southern China. As wages in Taiwan increase, wage-intensive industries, such as shoes and textiles, move to the mainland. Much of this activity is through Hong Kong intermediaries.

Two-way trade between Taiwan and the mainland exceeds twelve billion dollars a year.

8. Strategies for Economic Success

Reasons for Success

Why is Taiwan's economy so successful? Credit must be given to adept government planning. The first phase of growth, from 1953 to 1962, stressed the development of the infrastructure, improvement of agriculture, maintenance of price stability, and the development of industries to produce replacement products for imports. After 1962 the government emphasized intense industrialization. High technology receives current priority.

The economy can best be described as free-market capitalism with government economic control through ownership of basic industries. Taiwan's economy is skillfully guided by a well-educated bureaucracy. Investment is encouraged by a variety of incentives. The government is organized to make it as easy as possible to do business on the island.

Forms of Business Organization for Foreign Firms in Taiwan

Foreign investment is encouraged by allowing a wide variety of forms for business organization and by providing attractive tax incentives. Forms of business organization which are permitted are indicated in the following chart. Such a wide variety of business forms allows an

American corporation to choose an organization which best fits its goals, activities, and resources.

Taxation

The Republic of China started practicing "supply side" economics long before President Reagan ever mentioned the term. The tax structure is extremely favorable for foreign entrepreneurs. Income originating outside of Taiwan is not taxed. The tax policy is kept fluid to take advantage of changing economic conditions. It is always best to check for recent changes.

The taxable year is the calendar year. Upon approval business enterprises may adopt a fiscal year for tax purposes. Taxable income includes distributed profits and dividends, payments for services, interest, rent, sale of properties, and gambling winnings. All income obtained within the Republic of China is taxable.

Individual Income Tax

Individuals who reside in Taiwan for 183 days or more during a taxable year are subject to taxes. Nonresidents who stay for fewer than ninety days are subject to withholding on twenty percent of earnings from ROC sources but need not file an income tax return. Nonresidents who stay in Taiwan for more than ninety days but less than 183 days within a taxable year are required to file an income tax return and pay a twenty percent tax on earnings from ROC sources.

There are exemptions and deductions for charity, insurance, medical expenses, property taxes, casualty losses, and interest. Tax rates are progressive.

Business Taxes

Income taxes are levied upon all businesses physically located on Taiwan regardless of where management is located. If a firm is not physically operating on Taiwan it is not tax liable for goods and services sold on the island. The presence of a sales staff on Taiwan to sell goods or services makes a firm liable for business income taxes. Activities which do not involve sales of goods and services, such as purchasing and research, are exempt from business income taxes.

Valid business activities, within limits, are tax deductible. Provisions are allowed for deductions for percentages of losses on export sales, bad debts, foreign exchange losses, and payment of employee retirement benefits. Tax loss carry-forwards extend for three years. Deferred appreciation of fixed assets is available in certain loss situations upon approval of the ROC Ministry of Finance.

Special tax incentives are available to limited-by-shares businesses involved in exports, production, technology, international tourist hotels, and specialized technical services. A newly-formed firm which is eligible may select either accelerated depreciation of fixed assets or exemption from income tax for five years. Exemptions may also be obtained for investment in additional production equipment. Special situations may entitle a firm to investment tax credits and exemption from export duties.

All foreign production businesses are eligible for accelerated depreciation on replacement machinery or equipments, an income tax ceiling of twenty-five percent of taxable income, deductions for research expenses, depreciation based upon upward reevaluation of fixed assets in proportion to the wholesale price index, special provisions for losses on export sales, and special deductions for foreign exchange fluctuation losses on approved foreign currency loans to finance equipment expansion.

FORMS OF BUSINESS ORGANIZATION FOR FOREIGN FIRMS

Form	Allowed Activities	Requirements	Capital Contribution Required
Liaison office	Purchasing for head office	Registration of resident representative. Local or foreign.	None
Field office	Temporary office for completion of a particular contract.	Appointment of manager. Local or foreign.	None
Branch office	Service Trading Manufacturing	Foreign investment approval (FIA) to manufacture. Appointment of branch manager.	Remittance of foreign exchange capital contribution to Republic of China.
Local company (liability limited by shares)	Subsidiary in Republic of China	Seven registered stockholders. At least half of stockholders and chairman must be domiciled ROC nationals.	Minimum capital contribution of NT $1 million.
Local company (Limited liability without shares)	Subsidiary in Republic of China	Between five and twenty stockholders. At least half of stockholders and chairman must be domiciled ROC nationals.	Minimum capital contribution of NT $500, 000

Foreign Investment
Approval (FIA) Requirements

Only investments which have been approved by the
ROC Investment Committee may remit capital contribu-
tions and earnings out of the Republic of China. FIA capital investments may be made in the form of cash, equipment, raw materials, commodities, copyrights, patents,
or investment income or profits. FIA companies are also
exempt from certain limitations upon foreign capital and
management for local companies.

Eligibility for Foreign Investment Approval is limited
to companies contributing to the economic and social
development of Taiwan, firms involved in scientific and
technical research and development, large-scale trading
companies with share capital of NT $200 million or more,
major enterprises in communication, mining, and industry, or manufacturing for export or for identified and approved domestic needs.

Labor

Nowhere in the world can one find such trained and
industrious workers at such low cost. A shoe worker on
Taiwan earns about half percent of the wages of American shoe workers. It is no wonder that Taiwan is the major exporter of shoes to the United States.

Taiwan's work force consists of about ten million
people. Unemployment is about two percent. The government requires employers to contribute to occupational
training, so there are many skilled workers.

Wages and benefits have been rising as the result of a
short supply of labor rather than union militancy. The
government requires arbitration of all labor disputes; it
is illegal to strike.

Research and Technology

Taiwan's economic planners realize that cheap labor will not be an asset in the developing international post-industrial economy. So business and government are working together to achieve technological goals through research institutes such as the Institute of Information Industries and the Industrial Technology Research Institute.

The Science and Technology Advisory Group, headed by Minister K. T. Lin, has designated eight key areas for special attention: automation, biotechnology, electro-optics including lasers and precision instruments), energy (including nuclear power), elimination of Hepatitis B, the last prevalent contagious disease in Taiwan; improvement of food technology (including sanitation and packing), the development of synthetic materials to reduce imports, and the advancement of information systems technology to include computers and telecommunications.

Hsinchu Science Park

Taiwan is considered to be one of the "Four Little Dragons" of Asian technology. The government is determined that the Republic of China will surpass the others, Hong Kong, Singapore, and the Republic of Korea, in technological achievement. In order to transform Taiwan into a "big dragon" the government established a science park at Hsinchu, fifty miles south of Taipei, in 1980. Under Irving T. Ho, director-general of the park administration, over a thousand scientists and technicians are engaged in research and development of computers, lasers, and other space-age technologies. The Industrial Technology Research Institute and nearby universities provide academic support. Hsinchu Science Park uses Stanford University's industrial park as a model and is intended to raise Taiwan's technology to such a state-of-the-art that it will challenge California's Silicon Valley.

Domestic and foreign firms which are engaged in high-tech research and manufacturing are offered cheap land for purchase or free rental for five years. Other inducements to locate at Hsinchu include low cost financing, a five year tax holiday followed by a twenty-two percent tax ceiling, and government venture capital of forty-nine percent of total equity. Firms locating in the park are allowed to retain the option to buy back the government's forty-nine percent investment after the venture becomes profitable.

This technological push is already bearing fruit. American companies, such as Wang Laboratories, are using Taiwan as a technological base from which to compete with Japan. Industries already located at Hsinchu Science Park are involved in such areas as electronics, precision instruments, biological engineering, and material science. Current products include computer central processing units, peripherals, semiconductor devices, integrated circuits, microprocessors, computerized numerical control systems, silicon wafers, crystal resonators, robots, and laser scanners. High technology industries in Taiwan are so sufficiently developed that the government feels that some labor intensive industries are no longer needed. Timex was recently encouraged to move its watch assembly plant to the Philippines.

Domestic high-tech firms are also flourishing. Two Chinese companies located at the science park, Mitac, Inc., and Multitech International, are pioneering the development of Chinese language computer systems. Multitech's Dragon Computer system features an advanced Chinese language terminal invented by Chu Bang-fu. Taiwan's technological innovations are unique in Asia because they are undertaken by small entrepreneurs who lack the support of industrial giants as in Japan and Korea.

Export Processing Zones

In 1966 Taiwan established the first export process-ing zone (EPZ) in Asia at the southern port of Kaohsiung. Taiwan now has EPZs at Kaohsiung, Nantze, and Taichung.

An export processing zone is a designated area where firms, domestic and foreign, are allowed to build facto-ries, manufacture products, import raw materials, and export finished goods without duties or tariffs. EPZs pro-vide many inducements to foreign investors. There are no commodity or sales taxes. The Chinese government provides long-term loans for purchase and construction of factory buildings and for financing of exports and im-ports. Facilities for foreign exchange, warehousing, and transportation are modern, complete, and centralized. Utilities are inexpensive. Tax incentives and highly skilled but low cost labor complete the package of incentives. Some eighty thousand young single women work in Taiwan's EPZs. They live six to a room and pay rent of five dollars a month. Most are saving for dowries and work only a few years.

Kaohsiung's EPZ is located on about 168 acres of re-claimed land adjacent to the harbor. Security is tight. The zone is surrounded by a concrete wall topped with barbed wire. Foreign visitors must leave their passports at the gate. Chinese nationals must leave their identity cards. Mr. H. L. Chow, the public relations officer at Kaohsiung's EPZ was kind enough to lead me on a tour of the zone. Mr. Chow had formerly been stationed in Gabon on as-signment with a Republic of China agricultural team.

Over 130 firms are operating in the Kaohsiung EPZ. One of the most recent companies to locate in the zone was a South African firm involved in diamond cutting. The efficiency of the zone administration, the financial and tax inducements, and the lack of red tape have made this concept a great success.

To a person who is familiar with Asian history the godowns, which are warehouses near the dock, recall an earlier era. The immense success of these special zones seems ironic because they closely resemble the foreign enclaves which were forced upon China during the period of Western gunboat diplomacy in the 1830s.

The following chart lists industries which are eligible for admission to Taiwan's export processing zones.

INDUSTRIES ELIGIBLE FOR EPZ ADMISSION

Chemical products
Confectionery
Cosmetics
Educational materials/
  supplies
Electrical appliances
Electronic products
Furniture
Garments (non-cotton)
Handicrafts
Knitted and woven goods
  (non-cotton)
Leather products (except
  rawhide processing)
Medical instruments and
  accessories

Metal products
Musical instruments/
  supplies
Optical products
Paper containers
Plastic products
Precision machinery and
  instruments
Printed material
Rubber products
Sports gear and accesso-
ries
Toys
Transportation equipment
  and accessories
Yachts and mobile homes

---

9. *Economic and Business Problems*

Like all other dynamic economies, Taiwan's has problems. These relate to "pirating," accounting malpractices, "squeeze," wage escalation, the challenge of robotics, rising foreign trade protectionism, dependence on Mideast oil, population pressures, pollution, and cultural shock.

"Pirating"

Koxinga, Taiwan's famous pirate, was a "tiger" of a man. But the island's modern pirates are just copycats. For decades clever entrepreneurs have manufactured imitations of leading foreign products without paying royalties or copyright fees. The illegal goods include phony Levis, Adidas running shoes, Cartier watches, tapes, records, cosmetics, and computers. In addition to the manufacture of exact counterfeits complete with false labels the pirates manufacture "knock-offs" which closely resemble the real product. Fake Apple computers sell for about $350. Computers which are marketed as "IBM-compatible" are actually exact copies of IBM machines. At least the advertising is not false.

Although only a small part of Taiwan's production consists of pirated items this activity damages the reputation of the Republic of China's many legitimate industries.

Both the Republic of China and the United States have hardened their attitudes towards pirating in recent years.

The Chinese government has adopted a new trademark law and three company officials were recently convicted and sentenced to fourteen months in prison for counterfeiting Japanese sewing machines. In January, 1984, a Taiwanese district court sentenced six executives to eight months in prison for copying Apple software. Taiwan's Society for Industrial Automation and Automation Industries is addressing the problem of counterfeiting by helping local firms in international patent research.

In February, 1984, six people were indicted by a Philadelphia grand jury for smuggling counterfeit Apple computers into the United States. This was the first indictment of its kind in the United States. The same month the U.S. International Trade Commission ruled that Taiwanese computer makers had violated Apple patents by importing "Pineapple" and "Orange" computer counterfeits into the United States. In May 1992 the government passed a more stringent copyright law.

In spite of the above efforts counterfeiting is still rampant in Taiwan. Much still needs to be done.

Accounting Malpractices

There are no universally accepted accounting standards in Taiwan. Enforcement of company financial disclosure regulations is weak. Most Taiwanese companies keep three sets of books: one for the government, one for the bank, and one for the owners. Many taxes are evaded. Accounts receivable are often based upon sales projections rather than actual sales. Sometimes liabilities are not entered in financial records. Inventory may be overvalued or nonexistent. As the result of inadequate accounting and auditing practices both Chinese and foreign banks in Taiwan have suffered loan defaults.

During 1983, the Finance Ministry conducted an investigation of the books of all companies listed on the

Taiwan Stock Exchange. As a result several company officers were charged with illegal manipulation of financial records. Pai Pei-ying, Chairman of Taiwan's Security and Exchange Commission, stated that his investigations indicate that up to half of Taiwan's listed companies file inaccurate financial statements.

"Squeeze"

Since salaries are low in Taiwan "squeeze" is often needed to fulfill a person's financial obligations to his family. Almost everyone feels entitled to a "cut" of five or ten percent. Chinese look at this income as a type of commission. The problems arise when squeeze becomes excessive and when foreigners fail to understand this tradition. In some situations "squeeze" can be tantamount to extortion.

It is not possible to run modern businesses on the principle of "squeeze." Accounting becomes bedlam. The loyalties of "go-betweens" and other business representatives are always in doubt because these people may take a "cut" from both parties. No one is able to quantify the true cost or price of a product or service.

Wage Escalation

Wage levels in Taiwan are increasing at the rate of twenty to twenty-five percent per year. This is happening in spite of the fact that strikes are against the law. The economy is close to full employment and the large demand and small supply of labor pushes wages up. Many other nations of Asia, such as Indonesia, Malaysia, and the Philippines, now have wage rates lower than Taiwan's. The government of Taiwan must complete the transition to a technology-based economy soon because its labor-intensive products may soon be priced out of the market due to increased labor costs.

The Challenge of Robotics

Most American and Japanese firms in Taiwan have industrial robots on order. Robots manufactured by Teco Electric and Machinery Company, a local concern, are currently on the market. American executives in Taiwan realize that there is no such thing as a "cheap foreign robot." The steel collar workers produce just as economically in the United States. It is likely that many foreign companies will close their assembly lines in Taiwan when the use of robots becomes common at home. Only those American companies which can benefit from Taiwan's central location in East Asia or from special Taiwanese financial incentives are likely to stay. It is possible that considerable unemployment may occur in Taiwan as the result of the challenge of robots.

Rising Foreign Trade Protectionism

Taiwan's major export customers are demanding increased protection against the island's low-cost products. An example is the American color television industry. In June of 1983 the U.S. International Trade Commission found that American television manufacturers were being hurt by the dumping of color sets from Taiwan. Dumping occurs when imported goods are sold for less than the cost of production or for less than the domestic sales price. Taiwanese manufacturers dumped their television sets on the American market as an act of desperation because South Korea was surpassing Taiwan in sales to the United States.

Korea's television industry has advantages over Taiwan's because Korea's Big Three television manufacturers produce their own parts. In Taiwan some twenty companies assemble sets with parts provided by hundreds of manufacturing suppliers. Each company charges a markup to ensure itself a profit. In short, Taiwanese color television sets are becoming too expensive to compete on the world market.

This problem is not confined to Taiwan's color television industry. American manufacturers of shoes, steel, and copper frequently appeal for protection to the U.S. International Trade Commission. Powerful political pressure is exerted by American industries to raise the import barriers of Fortress America.

Dependence on Mideast Oil

Taiwan imports all of its oil. Eighty percent comes from Saudi Arabia and Kuwait. The island has been able to compensate for sharp oil price increases in the past by exporting more aggressively. But it is very vulnerable to closure of the Strait of Hormuz or an escalation of the war between Iran and Iraq. Sinkings of oil tankers in the Persian Gulf have ominous implications for Taiwan's economy.

The Government of the Republic of China is making every effort to diversify its sources of oil. But its main hope seems to be the expansion of nuclear power generation. Taiwan now obtains about a third of its energy from nuclear power. The island's third nuclear power plant, located near Kenting National Park in southern Taiwan, recently went into operation. By the year 2000 government planners expect to have twenty nuclear power reactors working. This will alleviate problems for industrial energy but do little to provide gasoline for the sharply increasing numbers of cars on the island.

Population Pressures

The population of Taiwan is now over twenty-one million. The island has less area than the Netherlands.

Since much of the land consists of uninhabitable mountains, population density is very high. Space is very limited. Yet there seems to be little control of population growth. If current trends continue the time will come when there will be no place to put the people.

Almost every Taiwanese family wants sons because only sons incur the obligation to support the parents in their old age. The government does not provide universal old age social security. Nevertheless, it tries to limit the number of children to two per couple. This is done through media campaigns.

Attitudes toward birth control are changing. In a recent televised panel discussion a group of young women frankly discussed the problems and procedures for effective birth control. Such frank expressions would not have been acceptable only a few years ago.

Pollution

Control of pollution has low priority for a nation which must produce and export at all costs in order to survive. Most large cities in Taiwan have badly polluted air due to uninhibited discharges from industrial smokestacks. Many rivers and streams are contaminated with chemicals.

At the present time most pollution is the result of industry. Since many people are buying cars for the first time automotive emissions will soon compound the problem. As in the West, environmental protection will probably not receive a high priority until the situation gets worse.

Cultural Shock

Many people in Taiwan face a dilemma because they want both the old tradition and the new technology.

Unfortunately the old and new ways of life are represented by separate economic-social-political packages from which people may not choose individual features. The old tradition calls upon man to harmonize with nature while the new technology exists only to bend nature to man. Tradition and change cannot coexist. For Chinese the greatest trauma comes from the terrifying realization that the great tradition must go.

10. How to Get Help in Doing Business in Taiwan

U.S. Business in Taiwan

U.S. commercial interest in Taiwan began in the 1850s, when American merchants in Canton established firms on the island. By 1967, the United States had eighty-two factories on Taiwan which were valued in excess of one hundred million dollars. By 1974 U.S. businesses had over five hundred million dollars invested in Taiwan. The total now is over three billion dollars.

One reason that the United States suffers a trade imbalance with Taiwan is because there is very little trade involvement by small and middle-size American firms. Yet there is a solid demand on the island for products which are manufactured by smaller American firms. Examples of these goods include medical instruments, cooking utensils and some items of clothing.

Much help is available to American firms seeking to do business with Taiwan. This assistance is not being used to its full potential. Sources of help include Chinese government agencies, businesses in Taiwan, U.S. government agencies, and businesses in the United States.

Addresses of these agencies and firms are listed in Chapter 15.

Assistance from the
Government of the Republic of China

A primary reason for Taiwan's economic success is the active assistance the government provides to foreign firms wishing to do business. Both the Coordination Council for North American Affairs (CCNAA) in New York and the Joint Industrial Investment Center in Taipei are organized for one-stop service. They make it easy to do business.

Coordination Council for
North American Affairs (CCNAA)

Since severance of diplomatic relations between the United States and the Republic of China the Coordination Council of North American Affairs has acted as an unofficial representative of Taiwanese interests in the United States. Offices are located in Atlanta, Chicago, Honolulu, Houston, Los Angeles, New York, San Francisco, and Seattle. The American Institute in Taiwan serves a similar function for the United States.

The Industrial Development
and Investment Center (IDIC)

The Industrial Development and Investment Center is designed to help foreign investors. It provides a broad range of services such as supplying information, arranging visits, and furnishing assistance in the preparation of investment applications. IDIC will send the following booklets upon request: *A Brief Introduction to the Investment Climate in Taiwan, Statute for Investment by Foreign Nationals,* and *Briefing on the Economic Progress in Taiwan.* This agency not only helps American businesses get established in Taiwan but acts as a troubleshooter for firms already located there.

The Joint Industrial
Investment Service Center (JIISC)

I visited the JIISC on Roosevelt Road in Taipei and was impressed by the quality of the staff. This office was established in 1982 to provide one-stop service to foreign investors. Its special mission seems to be to cut red tape. Assistance ranges from locating a manufacturing site to solving financing problems. The motto of JIISC rests on each person's desk: "Yes, We Can."

The China External Trade
Development Council (CETDC)

The China External Trade Development Council organizes trade shows. Many of these are held at its exhibition complex at Taipei Sung Shan Airport. This display center contains 1800 booths and 150 showrooms.

Taipei World Trade Center

The Taipei World Trade Center publishes a weekly booklet which includes lists of local businesses wishing to export and specifications of their products. Recent information on international trade and transportation is a feature of this publication.

Hsinchu Science Park
and Export Processing Zones

Administrations of Hsinchu Science Park and the export processing zones at Kaohsiung, Nantze, and Taichung will provide on-site briefings and send publications describing their operations upon request. The information provided includes financial incentives and requirements for admission.

ASSISTANCE FROM BUSINESSES IN TAIWAN

Consulting Services

There are a number of consulting services in Taiwan which offer a variety of services to American firms seeking to do business in Taiwan. They offer feasibility studies, credit reporting, market surveys, business planning, vocational training, and other services. Some companies specialize in assisting trade. The Overseas Buyers Service Center, the biggest private trade service company in Taiwan, will list an American company's needs in a monthly circular to over 20,000 suppliers in Taiwan.

Advertising Media

Advertising rates in Taiwan are reasonable and a variety of media are available. Newspaper advertising is very effective. There are about three dozen Chinese language newspapers on the island and the *China Post* and *China News* are published in English. Almost everyone has access to television so it is also a popular advertising medium. Theater-screen advertising is a particularly effective way to reach a young audience. Most Chinese love movies. Radio is also popular. There are more radio stations per capita in Taiwan than any other place in the world. Most magazines are too specialized for general-interest advertising.

Community Services Center

Taipei's Community Services Center, a non-profit community organization, addresses the needs of the English-speaking community for such activities as schools, health care, Chinese language instruction, and housing. It offers a free consultation.

American Banks in Taiwan

Many American banks have branches in Taipei. Among these are Bank of America, Chase Manhattan Bank, Chemical Bank, and Citibank. Some banks have formed trading companies in order to take advantage of the new American law and increase their effectiveness. A full list of American banks in Taiwan is included in Chapter 15.

Business Publications

The *Taiwan Buyer's Guide* contains alphabetical and classified lists of 15,000 local manufacturers, services, importers, exporters and industry associations. This guide is available through the Chinese Productivity Center.

The *Taiwan Yellow Pages* list over forty thousand manufacturers, importers, and service firms. This publication is available through the *China Post*.

Assistance from the U. S. Government

There are roughly 300,000 manufacturing firms in the United States. Few of these export. As a result the United States exports only about eight percent of its gross national product. This is about a third of the percentage of export for most other industrial nations.

American firms seem to be reluctant to use the help which is available from their government. Perhaps they fear red tape. But the services provided by U.S. Government agencies are timely, well-researched, effective, and often free.

American Laws Relating to Business with Taiwan

The Taiwan Relations Act was passed in 1979 to encourage business between Taiwan and the United States; it is known as Public Law 96-8.

The Economic Recovery Act of 1981 provided a much needed boost to Americans doing business abroad. Most are now exempt from double taxation. A portion of foreign-based income is free of U.S. taxes. To qualify, U.S. citizens must stay outside the United States at least 330 days in a twelve-month period.

American Institute in Taiwan (AIT)

The American Institute in Taiwan performs many of the functions formerly provided by our embassy in Taipei. AIT is a nonprofit corporation with offices in Arlington, Virginia and in Taipei and Kaohsiung in Taiwan. The institute also manages the American Trade Center in Taipei where it holds trade shows to promote American products.

The Department of Agriculture

The Department of Agriculture maintains trade offices overseas which help American business firms establish foreign contacts. In Taiwan the American Institute performs this function. Agriculture's Commodity Credit Corporation guarantees credit for approved exports. Help is available in locating overseas buyers and a direct mail service is available for American food exporters.

The Department of Commerce

The Department of Commerce sponsors investment and trade missions. Its *Market Share Reports* identify overseas markets. Commerce's Office of Major Contracts assists U.S. businesses in obtaining large foreign contracts.

World Data Reports, published by Commerce, provides credit information on almost 200,000 foreign firms.

For a fee of seventy-five dollars a firm can receive information on a specific foreign company.

Commerce publishes other helpful booklets such as *Marketing in Taiwan* and *Market Profiles for East Asia*. A report covering economic trends in Taiwan, prepared by the American Institute, is also available. Statistical data on trade with Taiwan is documented in reports titled *United States Trade with Major Trading Partners*.

The International Trade Administration

The International Trade Administration, an agency of the Department of Commerce, is organized into trade development sections specializing in such industry sectors as capital goods, consumer goods, transportation, and industrial goods and services. Its staff includes experts on every country in the world including communist nations. The International Trade Administration offers assistance ranging from export mailing lists to product marketing services. Another Commerce agency, the National Marine Fisheries Service, assists American businesses in exporting seafood.

The Agency for International Development (AID)

The Agency for International Development provides feasibility funding for trade, contracts, and investments abroad. It also funds banks which finance joint American and foreign products.

The Export-Import Bank

The Export-Import Bank develops America's export potential by encouraging small and medium-sized businesses to export goods and services. It offers an array of loans, guarantees, and insurance programs. The Foreign Credit Insurance Corporation acts as an agent for the Export-Import Bank to insure American exporters against non-payment by foreign buyers.

The Overseas Private Investment Corporation

The Overseas Private Investment Corporation is the key federal agency for encouragement of American business investment in developing nations. It furnishes feasibility funding, sponsors investment and trade missions, and provides insurance in case of currency inconvertibility, expropriation, war, or revolution. Direct loans and loan guarantees are available. This corporation publishes a 270 page reference manual titled *Washington's Best Kept Secrets: A U.S. Guide to International Business.* The Overseas Private Investment Corporation is a self-sustaining agency which has received no public funds since its initial appropriation.

The Small Business Administration (SBA)

The Small Business Administration guarantees export financing and is structured to meet the needs of the small business owner who plans to enter export markets for the first time. The SBA operates both management and financial assistance programs in accordance with Public Law 96-48 1.

The State Department

The State Department publishes bulletins which provide market leads. State's Office of Business and Export Affairs publishes information on strategies and risk evaluation for American businesses considering foreign operations.

The Office of U.S. Trade Representative

The Office of U.S. Trade Representative provides feasibility study funding for trade, contracts, and investment abroad. It also publishes information on commercial treaties and trade problems.

Local Agencies

State, county, and municipal agencies often have programs to assist firms in international business.

ASSISTANCE FROM AMERICAN BUSINESSES

Dun and Bradstreet

Dun and Bradstreet issues a publication titled *Principal International Businesses,* which lists credit information on fifty thousand firms in 133 nations.

U.S. Attorneys Specializing in Foreign Law

A list of attorneys who specialize in foreign law may be obtained from the International Trade Administration, Department of Commerce.

Trading Companies

A 1982 law allowing the formation of trading companies benefits small and medium-sized companies wishing to trade abroad. Firms can now join together to form export trading companies.

Some of the provisions of U.S. antitrust laws are now nullified for purposes of trading companies. The International Trade Administration will provide information on ways that firms can obtain protection from federal and state antitrust laws and will provide assistance in locating other firms interested in forming trading companies.

BankAmerica World Trade Corporation is an example of one of the new trading companies formed to implement the intent of the new law. BankAmerica World Trade Corporation offers a full range of services which include export, import, third country, and countertrade transactions. This company will take title to goods and act as a broker or joint venture partner. Other services relate to international transportation, insurance, and finance. A staff of area and product specialists provides expertise for international transactions.

11. Chinese and American Business Views of Each Other

Stereotypes and Fallacies

It takes so much time and energy to learn another culture that many people rely upon stereotypes which are based upon media or political influences.

The major contact between Chinese and Americans on Taiwan has been the result of business relationships although there has also been considerable academic and government interchange.

When Chinese and Americans look at each other they often share two common fallacies. One asserts that there are no real differences between Chinese and Americans, "Both are human." The other states that there are such great differences between the two societies that Chinese and Americans must be entirely different. In reality all humans share a common nature but that nature is conditioned quite differently by their respective cultures.

American stereotypes of Chinese have ranged from the clever Charlie Chan to the evil Fu Man Chu. The common view that Chinese are inscrutable is false. They are actually very open and emotional. The Chinese reputation for inscrutability began when the first Chinese to enter the United States, like any other immigrants in a strange culture, withdrew into their own communities.

Chinese stereotypes of Americans stem from the ethnocentric nature of Chinese culture. Because China had the only high civilization in its part of the world for so many years, its people looked down on all other societies. Since China had the only great seminal culture in its part of the world all foreigners were viewed as barbarians. Some Chinese still feel the United States is too young to have a culture. One who understands Mandarin can hear little children refer to him with such pejoratives as "red-haired devil" and "long-nosed one."

Favorable Chinese stereotypes of Americans were formed as the result of American missionary work in Taiwan and the island's receipt of economic and military aid. American technology is viewed as the world's best.

Favorable Chinese Views of Americans

The Chinese on Taiwan have some positive opinions of Americans. We are viewed as having lots of money and being informal, friendly, and carefree. Many Chinese believe that all Americans are rich. These concepts are reinforced by American movies and TV programs which are very popular in Taiwan.

Japan and the United States are Taiwan's biggest trading partners. It is natural for businessmen to compare visitors representing these two nationalities. A leading Taiwanese industrialist stated that "American businessmen are as broad-minded as their country, whereas Japanese businessmen are as narrow-minded as their islands. Japanese are by nature, industrious, patriotic, and skeptical. They learn, imitate, and surpass. But they never let others learn from them. But American businessmen will share their technology."

The Chinese on Taiwan believe that Americans are easy to handle. When Vice President Agnew visited the island our amah was visited by the police and told to report at a certain street corner an hour before the parade to greet Agnew. The route of the parade went down the most modern street in Taipei. Uniformed police handed out little American flags to a crowd which had been coerced to attend. Our Vice President returned with glowing reports about how much the Taiwanese liked the United States.

Perhaps the greatest compliment that the Chinese pay to Americans is the desire many Chinese have to move to the United States. This wish seems to be motivated by economic considerations and the relative safety of living in a nation which is a world power rather than by a wish for more freedom. Most Chinese on Taiwan believe that American society has too much freedom and too little order.

Negative Chinese Views of Americans

While Chinese admire American economic and business success they have some negative opinions of individual American traits. Americans seem to be wasteful. The thick newspaper Americans buy every Sunday and throw out every Monday would provide a typical Chinese family with wrapping paper for several weeks. Our consumption of so much meat, milk, and cheese makes us smell a little like animals to Chinese. Even Chinese dogs, oxen, and water buffalo seem to notice the difference and may become violent when they pick up the scent of Westerners.

Americans also have the reputation for violence. The villain in Chinese literature and movies is usually tall with blue eyes, a long nose, and light hair. Chinese animated television cartoons also reflect this stereotype. Americans are often viewed as being individualistic, violent, impulsive, and uncultured. American television programs, shown widely in Taiwan, reinforce this concept.

Many Chinese feel that American businessmen look at them only as a means of making money. The American approach to business seems to be too brusque, a form of brutal efficiency that overrides human relations. One of the most common complaints of the Chinese business-men I spoke with in Taiwan was that Americans only call or visit them when they have something to sell. They pre-fer that both personal and business relationships be more continuous and broader in scope.

The president of a shoe manufacturing company in Taichung told me that "American business people are not stable. They go for the lowest price even if the quality is poor. We are not able to maintain stable long-term rela-tionships with American businesses." Other Chinese busi-nessmen also stated that the emphasis on price disturbed them. They felt that American businessmen ignored fac-tors other than price, such as quality, dependability, and delivery time. The Chinese business system values close and continuous relationships even when there are some short-term disadvantages. They feel that the willingness to help the other party in the short term often results in long-term benefits for themselves.

Chinese seem to find Americans to be very puzzling because there seems to be no norm. The rules of Ameri-can society do not restrict human behavior as narrowly as Chinese social rules. American society is more diverse and includes people of many ethnic backgrounds. There are idealistic, rude, friendly, avaricious and religious Americans. All kinds.

Favorable American Views of Chinese

Almost all the American businessmen I spoke with in Taiwan viewed their Chinese counterparts as hard work-ing, frugal, respectable, and family-oriented. These at-tributes are very similar to the Protestant Ethic which is a basic value for American business.

Chinese seem to have a love for life and a capacity for happiness even under difficult circumstances. Americans on Taiwan often remarked that they appreciated the Chinese wit. Chinese humor often rests on the ability to laugh at oneself. Anyone who has seen Chinese enjoying the "finger-game," a variation of our "sticks and stones," has wondered at the simple enjoyments of Chinese life.

Chinese hospitality is also a strong point. There seems to be no limit to Chinese efforts to please a guest. During my recent visit to Taiwan I was a house guest of a Taiwanese businessman. When he discovered that the bed was too short for me he insisted that I move to a hotel for the night. He paid the hotel bill in advance so I was unable to pay my own bill. If you are a guest of a Chinese you will find that you will be unable to pay for your own meals, lodging, transportation, tobacco, liquor, or entertainment.

Negative American Views of Chinese

One of my contacts was an American businessman who markets chemicals in Taiwan, Korea, and Hong Kong. He works through Chinese agents in Taiwan and was having great difficulties. If his agents made mistakes they always refused to admit them. An American would simply say, "I dropped the ball." But Chinese never want to be confronted with a mistake because it would mean "loss of face." This businessman also found it difficult to deal directly with Chinese agents. They always seemed to "go around" a problem rather than confronting it directly. He thought the people who worked for him were evasive and he was anxious to return to the United States.

Another American I spoke with was visiting Taiwan to buy receiving units for satellite dishes. He arrived in Taipei only a few weeks after making an appointment with a Chinese firm. In the meantime the firm had apparently gone out of business. The officers of the firm did not notify him of this fact so he could cancel his trip. He was very upset because his contacts "no longer existed." He felt that Taiwan had too many small companies which were underfinanced and the idea of doing business on the island simply "scared" him. He had just about decided to do business with a Korean firm because companies in Korea are larger and more dependable "like the Japanese."

By Western standards Chinese seem to exhibit a strange incongruity. A snapshot I have of a Chinese friend shows him sitting in his favorite chair, wearing his best suit, and assuming his most dignified pose. The shade of the lamp next to his chair is tilted at a very extreme angle. He knew the shade was unbalanced but was insensitive to its effect on the aura he wanted the photo to display. To Americans many aspects of Chinese life are like this.

12. *Etiquette and Bargaining*

Gifts

When visiting a Chinese host, presentation of a gift is in order. Taiwan has high taxes on foreign luxury goods so almost anything imported is appreciated. Bring such items as Scotch, bourbon, brandy, perfumes, cigarettes, chocolates, fine cloth, or ginseng. Most of these can be purchased at airport duty-free shops prior to your departure.

Gifts should be offered with both hands. Your host will probably not open your gift in your presence. This custom is designed to avoid embarrassment to you if the gift is not particularly expensive or appropriate.

At a Chinese wedding it is expected that guests will bring a gift of money wrapped in a small red envelope.

Potential Areas for Misunderstanding

The Chinese perception of social relations involves multiple layers of meanings. It is easy for a westerner to give offense without meaning to do so. As a house guest of a Chinese friend I once searched my pockets for my pipe. My host immediately responded by saying that "Everyone is honest here."

It is easy to commit a faux pas by omission; always inquire about the health of your counterpart's family.

Introductions can sometimes be confusing when a Chinese decides to call himself by his given name first, Western style. My visa to the Republic of China was once delayed because the Chinese consulate in Hawaii had my record filed under my first name.

It is considered polite to demean yourself and your possessions. However, when your host refers to his house as a hovel or to himself as uneducated do not agree with him. You should respond by demeaning yourself and praising him. But do not express admiration for a possession since he is obligated by custom to give you an object you praise.

Meals and Entertaining

Chinese businessmen will seldom entertain in their homes. Most of their houses are too small; only the wealthy have large homes. Instead, they will take you to a restaurant. If you should be invited to a Chinese house you will usually find that the wife spends most of her time in the kitchen because meals are served serially. Do not appeal to the wife to join you because that is the Chinese way.

The Chinese in Taiwan are becoming accustomed to Western ways and will sometimes entertain informally. But many still choose a traditional Chinese banquet in which a knowledge of Chinese table manners will help you impress your host.

At formal dinners the speech may precede the meal. Toasts will often be offered at this time. The place settings on the round tables will not include knives because they are considered to be weapons. The food will already have been cut to bite-size pieces. The only utensils needed are chopsticks and a Chinese spoon for the soup. If you are the guest of honor you will likely be placed to the left of the host. If chicken is served you will be offered the head. Chicken brains are considered to be a delicacy.

The meal will begin with cold dishes. It is best not to eat these unless you are sure of sanitary preparation. It is safe to eat anything hot from the wok or oven. Chinese food offers much variety. A banquet usually consists of as many dishes as there are diners plus soup and rice. Dishes are served family-style. Although your host will probably put food on your plate with his chopsticks, you are free to help yourself. Do not dig with your chopsticks into the serving dishes to get the tastiest morsels because that is considered impolite. If you do not leave a little food in each serving dish and on your plate, your host is obligated to have more food prepared.

A Chinese banquet will include a delightful array of meat, vegetables and seafoods. There will be no milk or cheese since Chinese obtain their calcium from cook-softened bones and greens. Sometimes it is best not to ask your host the nature of the dishes. Eel, snake, and dog meat become delicacies when they enter the Chinese cuisine. One province specializes in dried rat meat.

Table manners are entirely different in China. You may lift your rice or food bowl to your mouth to shorten the distance necessary to shovel the food with your chopstick. Since it is considered unsanitary to take bones, shrimp shells, gristle, and seeds from your mouth with your hands, it is permissible to spit them on the floor or tablecloth.

It is considered polite to slurp your noodles or soup. The more noise you make in doing this the greater appreciation you show for the meal. Take extra ties, shirts, and suits to Taiwan and do not wear your best to banquets. No meal is considered a success unless clothes and tablecloths are well splattered with food.

Warm wine will be served in small cups. This will likely be the sherry-flavored yellow Shaohsing or the fiery Kaoliang. Always hold the cup with two hands, one under, one around. When you are toasted you need only take a sip of wine unless your host says "Kan-bei" (dry cup), then it is bottoms up on one gulp. If each

Chinese counterpart toasts you separately it is difficult to keep pace!

Soup and fish are served toward the end of the meal although soup may be served several times during the banquet. Additional servings of rice, noodles, or tea may signal that the banquet is over. Toothpicks are usually provided and you may pick your teeth at the table as long as you cover the sight of this activity with one hand. Once you leave the table it is time to go home. Chinese do not linger at the end of a meal.

If you plan to be the host at a restaurant be sure to pay the bill before the meal begins. Otherwise, all the Chinese present will enjoy a loud squabble as each tries to pay. It is the custom for the hosts to see the guests to their cars or cabs.

Preludes to Bargaining

It is essential that you obtain a letter of introduction or a personal introduction from a mutual friend, business acquaintance, or bank. Chinese businessmen want to know who you are, your business background, and your family origin. Always present your business card when being introduced. To Chinese, American businessmen often seem to be too glib. Westerners often arrive at a first name relationship within minutes of meeting while Chinese will usually address friends of many years as "mister." Friendships are not made lightly because they involve many obligations. A good friend is considered an extension of the family.

Selling Yourself

You will have to sell yourself before you can market your product or service. Taiwanese businessmen must be convinced that they can trust you. They will want to view your behavior under a variety of situations and determine whether you are well regarded by your peers, superiors, and subordinates. It may take many days of contacts in order to develop mutual respect and understanding. You will succeed or fail in your business goals on the basis of your Chinese counterpart's evaluation of you as a person. Your character will be a more important factor in your business dealings than any contract or legal agreement. You must develop a genuine human relationship separate from any business context. This will likely involve after-hours associations such as sharing entertainment, cultural and sporting events, and dinners. Thoughtful gifts may help establish the trust and friendship needed for close business relationships.

In Taiwan business is a male domain. A night out for after-hours socializing is designed to establish camaraderie, so leave your wife at home or at the hotel. Bar hostesses and nightclub entertainers often represent the Taiwanese adaptation of the Japanese geisha. Although prostitution exists, the flirting that occurs may not be much different from conduct at American conventions.

Sometime during this process of getting to know each other business topics will likely enter the discussion. Your counterpart will do this in a subtle and informal way. Your response should also be subtle and informal. Do not call up your lawyer or pull out a contract at this point.

"Yes," "Maybe," and "No."

There are no exact translations between languages. The same word in different cultures may have entirely different connotations. "Yes" to a Chinese often means "I understand you," not agreement. "Maybe" usually means "no." Chinese believe it to be impolite to disagree. Smooth relationships are valued more than frankness. When you have a difficulty understanding your counterpart's responses, get a reliable third party, perhaps the person who originally introduced you, to find out what "yes," "no," and "maybe" really mean in this particular situation.

Intentional Communication Difficulties

Find out beforehand how well your counterpart speaks English. He may feign lack of understanding and ask for a translation to Chinese in order to give him time to think of a reply or he may ask you to repeat often in order to wear you down. You would not be the first American businessman to be asked to repeat a long and detailed presentation because your Chinese counterparts did "not understand it the first time." They know that second and third presentations are always less enthusiastic.

Appointments

Chinese and Americans have different concepts of business and social obligations. People of other cultures often look at American pinpoint punctuality as something brutally efficient. Try not to be offended if your counterpart is late or fails to appear. Perhaps he did not want to agree to the appointment but had no way to say "no."

Bargaining Techniques

Chinese are good negotiators because bargaining is a common activity for them. Your counterpart has more practice because he is accustomed to bargaining for nearly everything. While Americans usually bargain only for houses and cars, Chinese negotiate for almost anything. Prices on Taiwan are often based on the ability to pay.

Your Chinese counterpart is sure to ask you what you paid for your watches, shoes, clothes, and other possessions. He will do this because he needs to know the value of things for bargaining. You too will need to learn about the value of things and ability to pay.

Americans usually bargain for clear-cut goals such as price, quality, or delivery date. Chinese objectives are more subtle. Your counterpart may be concerned about the effect of your agreement upon his long-term relationships with his suppliers or bank.

It is best to keep your options open on as many points as possible for as long as you can. This not only increases your counterpart's stress but allows you to retain more flexibility. It is usually best to save negotiation of the toughest point until the end. It may be easier to handle after everyone has consumed a lot of time and energy.

An American broadcasting executive who had many years of experience in dealing with Chinese told me that "Asians have infinite patience. They usually win." Asians certainly know how to use time to their advantage. During the negotiations to end the Vietnam War, it took years to get the North Vietnamese to the bargaining table. When they finally arrived in Paris, they rented a villa on a two-and-a-half year lease. The American delegation, expecting a shorter conclusion, stayed at a hotel and paid by the week.

If you plan to use time to your own advantage, never disclose your deadline. If you are visiting Taiwan to close a contract it may be best not to make a return air reservation until your deal has closed. If you do your counterpart will soon know your deadline. Give him a date earlier than your real deadline for completion of negotiations and you will find that most of his concessions will occur after your false deadline.

Finally, be careful about discussing important aspects of your negotiating strategy. For may years the fourth floor of a leading business hotel in Taipei was wired so the hotel could sell Western business secrets to Chinese firms. Never assume the confidentiality of phones, telex, and mail. The Chinese became masters of intrigue long before the West had a culture. Few secrets can survive in Taiwan.

PART THREE

The Personal Experience

This handbook is not intended to be a tourist guide but I have included information which should increase the enjoyment of your visit.

There will be considerable overlap between your personal and business activities. Your adjustment to Taiwan and your understanding of its people will enhance your business effectiveness.

13. Travel Tips

Preparation

A visa is required to enter Taiwan. Applications should be directed to the Republic of China's Coordinating Council for North American Affairs. Local addresses are listed in Chapter 15. A tourist visa is good for sixty days and permits multiple entries. A business or resident visa is needed for longer stays.

No health shots are required for admission to Taiwan. Hepatitis B is prevalent on the island and you may wish to check with your physician since a vaccine is now available. It is always a good idea to keep your tetanus shots up to date no matter where you are. Cholera, yellow fever, or typhus shots may be required for entrance to Taiwan if you travel via an area which is undergoing an outbreak of one of these diseases. Some types of shots need to be taken in series so plan well in advance if you are going to take them.

The humidity in Taiwan is nearly always high. Depending upon the season the weather on the island is either chilly and wet or hot and wet. Bring a plastic raincoat and an umbrella. If you have a choice of seasons for a business trip, go between March and May or in October or November. Typhoons are common from June through September.

A plastic water flask can be handy since tap water is not safe to drink without boiling or treatment. Small first-aid and sewing kits can save time and trouble. If you will

be changing locations frequently, wash and wear clothes
are worth taking. Business activities require suits, double
knit or blends will save pressing problems.

Departure

It is best not to exchange American money into New
Taiwanese dollars at your departure airport in the United
States. The exchange rate at San Francisco International
was 24 NT for $1 US. At the airport in Taipei, the rate was
nearly 26 NT for $1 US. Take small denominations of
traveler's checks and American dollars for use until you
get money exchanged.

Duty-free shops at U.S. airports and aboard planes over
the Pacific offer bargains. Prices at such shops in Asian airports are usually high. The duty-free shop at your departure airport is a good place to buy gifts to present to your
business associates in Taiwan. Most of these shops do not
provide gift wrapping. Take along some gift paper and
scotch tape in order to save yourself the problem of finding these after arrival. The Republic of China allows you to
bring in one bottle of alcoholic spirits, two hundred cigarettes, and a small bottle of perfume duty-free. The same
limits apply to duty-free items brought back to the United
States. Be sure to register the serial numbers of foreign-
made possessions at your departure airport so you will
not have to pay duty on these when you re-enter the United
States. Customs form 4457 is required for this purpose.

En Route

Your trans-Pacific flight will take at least ten hours
and you will lose a day on your westward flight if you are
in the air at midnight. Your air ticket and itinerary will
refer to local times but this will not alleviate your jet lag.
There is a sixteen-hour time difference between Taiwan

and the west coast of the United States. Eight P.M. on Monday in San Francisco is noon Tuesday in Taiwan.

Arrival

Taipei International Airport is located eighteen miles southwest of Taipei. Chinese customs are usually lenient to citizens of the United States.

You should declare radios, TV sets, cameras, and type-writers when you enter Taiwan and save the form to facilitate your departure. Keep receipts of dollars exchanged for Chinese money so you can reconvert at your time of departure. Unlimited U.S. currency may be brought into the Republic of China but it must be declared upon arrival to be taken out of Taiwan. If you do not save your currency declaration and exchange receipts, you will only be allowed to take US $1,000 out of Taiwan. There is no limit on traveler's checks but only NT $8,000 may be brought in or taken out of the country.

A tourist map is available at the airport which identifies locations in both English and Chinese. Transportation by cab or bus is available to downtown Taipei. Gray Line buses run to several hotels and the Chung-hsin Line charges a nominal fare for a trip to the domestic airport which is near downtown Taipei.

Overcoming Jet Lag

When you arrive in Taiwan your body will follow the time in the United States. One's circadian rhythm will not accept such an abrupt time change. What can one do to alleviate jet lag? If you arrive in the morning take a two or three hour nap as soon as you arrive at the hotel. Then enjoy a light lunch. If you arrive in the evening resist the need to sleep until your normal bed time. If you go to sleep too early you will find it difficult to adjust to the local time. If you eat and drink lightly while you are in the air you will suffer less after you land.

Minimizing Costs

According to figures compiled by Business International Corporation, Taipei is one of the ten most expensive cities in the world. A total of ninety-three cities were surveyed. This study addresses itself to the costs of living in Taipei at an American standard. Taipei can be a very inexpensive city to visit or live in if you are able to adjust somewhat to indigenous standards.

Cabbies, money exchangers, merchants, and service people in Taiwan are no different than their counterparts anywhere in the world. Your wallet will suffer "the death of a thousand cuts" unless you are careful. Cabbies will try to charge twice the approved rate for the trip from the airport to Taipei. Conversions between systems of measurements also offer opportunities for dishonesty. The following chart should be helpful.

The custom of tipping is not as widespread as in the United States. A ten percent service charge will be added to your bill by hotels and restaurants so if you tip you will pay twice. It is not customary to tip taxi drivers. People who carry your baggage or are especially helpful should receive some small change.

Units of Measurement

Chinese	American
1 Catty (used for food)	1-1/3 Pounds
1 Meter	about 40 Inches
1 Liter	Slightly more than a Quart
1 Kilometer	About 5/8 of a Mile
1 Kilogram.	2-1/5 Pounds
1 Hectare	2-1/2 Acres
30 Grams	1 Ounce

Hotels

Taiwan has a wide range of hotels with daily room charges ranging from US $20 to over US $200. A list of hotels with addresses is included in Chapter 15. The Grand Hotel and The Ritz have top reputations. At the Grand one has the feeling of being the guest of an emperor. Its upswept roof, gold trim, and red pillars reflect the architectural grandeur of ancient China.

Most American appliances will operate on Taiwan's 100 volt A.C. electricity. During typhoons electricity is often shut off to avoid fires caused by damaged lines.

Living in Taiwan

If you are assigned to live in Taiwan you will find that you can live at an American level for about the same cost as in New York. It costs much less to live at a Chinese level. Servants are plentiful and inexpensive. Minor irritations include the need to boil water and treat salad greens with a Chlorox solution before serving. Some Americans miss fine bakery goods which are difficult to find on the island.

Most Americans I met on Taiwan said that they had adjusted readily although they suffered a short period of cultural shock.

Getting Around in Taiwan

Taxis are plentiful and inexpensive. It is not customary to tip cabbies. The only problem is communication. Cabbies do not read or speak English and a few do not read Chinese. Ask your hotel desk clerk to write your destination in Chinese or carry a map that identifies locations in both English and Chinese. Carry your hotel's card so you can show its address to a cabbie in order to get back. Rental cars are now available in Taiwan. Unless you enjoy driving in chaotic traffic, it is better to rent a private car with driver or take a cab.

Public travel in Taiwan is efficient and inexpensive. Avoid travel during the Chinese New Year because Chinese return to their homes at this time and you can easily become stranded. The express trains are comfortable and make the trip between Taipei and Kaohsiung in about four hours. Bus service is available all over the island. Departures are frequent and the fare between Taipei and Kaohsiung is less than US $15. Reserved seat tickets may be purchased two days in advance. Few train or bus ticket agents speak English. Unless you speak some Mandarin, buy tickets through a travel agency or take a Chinese friend with you.

Domestic air travel is excellent and you can fly anywhere on the island in less than an hour. Sung Shan, Taipei's domestic airport, is only three miles from downtown.

Communications

Taiwan has one of the world's best postal systems. Air mail letters to the United States take four or five days. Overseas phone calls can be made through arrangements with your hotel.

Health Precautions

Cities in Taiwan often experience water shortages due to insufficient pumping capacity and heavy usage. The suction created in underground pipes sucks in contaminated ground water. So never drink raw tap water. Drink only bottled liquids, tea, or water that has been boiled or treated. If a cup or glass looks dirty do not use it. Hepatitis is endemic on Taiwan.

Food and beverages at the international standard hotels are as safe as those served at similar hotels anywhere in the world. Elsewhere avoid salads (which may have been fertilized with night soil) and cold foods (which may have been visited by flies). Eat only food which is hot from the wok or oven. Fruit with skin is safe to eat if the skin is unbroken.

Hepatitis may be transmitted by unsanitary dishes or utensils. I have seen Chinese bring a clean cloth to a restaurant in order to wipe the dishes and utensils before dining. One can see blocks of ice resting on sidewalks which are used by children to relieve themselves.

If you do become sick the island has an adequate number of excellent hospitals. Normal precautions should be sufficient. I lived in Taipei for three years and was never ill.

Tobacco and Alcohol

Tobacco and alcohol are available for sale from the Taiwan Tobacco and Wine Monopoly Bureau. Addresses of these outlets are listed in Chapter 15. Stores sell these products but the tobacco may be old and the liquor may not be authentic.

Departure

Your airline will want you to report at the airport several hours early. There is a small departure fee which must be paid at the time you check your baggage.

U.S. Customs

You are allowed to bring back $400 worth of foreign purchases duty free. If you stay outside the United States over thirty-one days this goes up. If you exceed the limit you will have to pay a ten percent duty on the first $600 of excess over the $400 exemption. At this point it gets more complicated and it is best to check with customs if you plan extensive purchases. Write for information concerning the Generalized System of Preferences. For major purchases of more than $250 always get a certificate of origin when you purchase the item. There is an IRS tax on liquor over one bottle. Articles purchased abroad and mailed to the United States are subject to duty if valued at $50 or more. It is a good idea to pack your purchases in a separate suitcase to avoid delay at customs. Customs is usually understanding about product samples.

14. Things to Do, See, and Learn

Be a Part-time Tourist

Be sure to take time out from your business schedule to see Taiwan. Your excursions will be enjoyable and you will gain knowledge you will be able to use in your business activities on the island. The Taiwan Visitor's Association publishes a monthly booklet which is free at all major hotels. This publication is a good source of up-to-date information regarding tourist activities.

Chinese Foods and Beverages

One of the best opportunities one has in Taiwan is the availability of the world's most varied and delectable cuisine. Chinese seem to be preoccupied with food. The standard greeting is "Have you eaten yet?"

Most Americans think of Cantonese cooking when they think of Chinese food. This is due to the fact that most Chinese in the United States came originally from Canton. Yet China has many provincial styles of cooking and all of them are represented by restaurants in Taiwan which were founded by refugees from all over the Chinese mainland.

In the entire northern half of China rice is not grown; wheat is the staple. So you will find many restaurants in Taiwan which feature noodles, breads, dumplings, buns, and rolls.

An American who says that "Chinese food doesn't fill me up" simply has not consumed enough rice. Except at banquets, meat and vegetables are served in quantities only sufficient to flavor the rice. Chinese usually eat three or more bowls of rice at a meal. Chinese often cannot "fill up" on American food because they do not eat sufficient quantities of potatoes and bread.

The character of Chinese cuisine is conditioned by chronic shortages of both food and fuel. The wok represents the best design for cooking food quickly with as little fuel as possible. No waste is allowed. Almost anything that can be eaten *is* eaten. Sea cucumbers, sea slugs, and chicken feet, under the care of a Chinese chef, become delicacies.

In China's ancient dynasties the court chef had to prepare one-hundred course meals for the emperor. If he ever repeated a dish he was beheaded and a more imaginative cook was hired. This custom stimulated great creativity and helped to produce a Chinese culinary tradition which has great range and unbelievable variety. It also encouraged the practice of using euphemisms to make every dish appear different. A spinach and crabmeat dish becomes "green jade and red coral." Large meatballs are named "lion's head." Cat and snake are served as "tiger and dragon." Dog becomes "fragrant meat."

Some of the best Chinese foods are designed to be served as snacks. One of my favorites is jowdz. These steamed dumplings are called "pot-stickers" when fried. They are made of chopped pork, cabbage, green onions, and ginger in a half-moon shaped dough wrapper. When dipped in a mixture of soy sauce, sesame oil, vinegar, and hot pepper oil, jowdz tastes superb. My wife learned to prepare it and jowdz is frequently on our table.

Mongolian barbeque also pleases the Western palate.

The diner selects beef, venison, wild boar, or lamb. He dips the meat in a sauce of his own making and grills it over a fire.

Peking duck is probably the most famous northern Chinese dish. Air is blown under the duck's skin with straws to make it extra crispy when baked. The skin is inserted in a wrapper with a scallion and brown plum sauce, rolled up and eaten. The duck meat, soup, and fat are served in separate dishes. The duck fat is beaten with eggs, chopped scallions, and bits of ham to create a great dish.

Some of China's greatest essays were written about famous banquets. Fine cuisine on Taiwan comes from many provincial traditions. The following chart should be a helpful guide.

Tea is served with Chinese meals. There are many grades of tea as well as many types. Green tea is not fermented. Oolong tea is half fermented. Black tea is fully fermented. All taste good.

Shao-hsing wine is made from rice. It is somewhat sweet and salty, yellow in color, and is usually served hot. Kaoliang wine is stronger and is made from sorghum. It has a high alcoholic content and the kick of vodka. Taiwan produces good rum but it is not promoted.

Provincial Cooking Styles

Province	Style	Examples
Cantonese	Colorful, sweet	Spring rolls, steamed dumplings
Fukienese, Taiwanese	Mild. Steamed and stewed dishes	Stewed fish, delicious soups
Hunanese (Central China)	Very, very hot steamed dishes	Sweet and sour carp Steamed chicken
Mongolian	Barbeque	Wild game, lamb
Peking (North China)	Mild. Noodles and bread	Peking duck, Sour and hot soup. Eel, chicken
Shanghai (Eastern China)	Mild seasoning	Braised shark fin. Eels, prawns; many seafoods
Szechuan (Western China)	Spicy, red hot chilies	Prawns, oxtail soup. Roast duck with camphor leaves

Restaurants

Unless you know what to order, hotel restaurants are not usually the best places to go for Chinese food. Their menus are designed to be bland for the tourist palate. Many authentic Chinese restaurants have dingy appearances. They prefer to put their energies into cuisine rather than ambiance. In recent years numerous international restaurants have opened in Taiwan. A list of restaurants with addresses is included in Chapter 15.

Shopping

Taiwan offers many products for shoppers but there is less variety than in Hong Kong. Lacquerware is excellent in quality and low in price. Brassware includes beds which are designed to be shipped unassembled. Marbleware, produced in Hualien, includes items from vases to fireplaces. Taiwan's jade was depleted years ago. Jade sold in Taiwan comes from British Columbia. Watch out for plastic or glass jade imitations.

Throughout history the Chinese have used bamboo for every conceivable purpose. Stores in Taiwan feature bamboo items from fishing poles to handbags. A variety of furniture is available in rattan, wood, bamboo, and metal. Rugs and carpets for sale include the famous Tientsin type. Other products include woodcarvings, coral, cloisonné, screens, dolls, toys, and glassware.

Ran In Tang's paintings are highly regarded and sell for hundreds of dollars. Chen Yang-chun's watercolors usually focus on rural scenes. He has his own gallery on Kwanfu Road in Taipei.

Custom-tailored men's suits are priced from US $150, shirts from US $12. The Chi pao, with the traditional slit skirt and high collar, is a specialty of some tailors.

Pirated items, especially books, records, and tapes, are available for sale at about one-third the price of the authentic items. Pirated items are not supposed to be taken out of Taiwan.

Bargaining

If you enjoy bargaining you will enjoy shopping in Taiwan. Fixed prices are found only at government operated or approved stores. The rules of bargaining are classic. Never let the shop owner know which item interests you most. Never pay the first price. Offer about half the asking price and bring your offer up as the shopkeeper brings his price down.

Taiwanese shops will ask for different prices based upon the shopkeeper's perception of your ability to pay, your knowledge of Mandarin or Taiwanese, and your nationality. Always maintain a smile and negotiate in good humor.

Taipei: Cultural Activities

The Confucian Temple, located at Chiu Chuan Street, just off Chung Shan North Road, is worth seeing. Ceremonies are held here on Confucius' birthday, September 28. Lung Shan Temple, called the Temple of Dragon Hill, is located on Hsi Yuan Road in the Wan Hwa area of southwest Taipei. It was constructed in 1738 and is probably the oldest Buddhist temple in Taipei. Snake meat, said to be good for health, is sold from carts in nearby alleys. Taipei Mosque serves the religious needs of the city's Moslems and is one of the most impressive mosques in East Asia. It is located at 62 Hsinsheng South Road.

The National Palace Museum (Chung Shan Museum) houses the most important collection of Chinese art in the world. Some 300,000 art objects were transported under wartime conditions from the mainland to Taipei. Exhibits include bronze and jade items, paintings, pottery, and religious articles. Some of these took the efforts of several generations of a family to produce. Lectures are available twice a week. A person would have to visit this museum many times over many years to see all the articles in the vast collection.

Check the Chinese Armed Forces Cultural and Activity Center for times of opera performances. The Provincial Botanical Gardens on Hoping West Road feature tropical plants. The National Central Library and National Historical Museum are located nearby. Other interesting sights include the historical museum at Academia Sinica,

Taipei New Park with its Provincial Museum, and the Presidential Office Building on the site of the Double Tenth military parades.

Taipei: Sports

Taipei offers much to the golfer. There are seven golf courses within a half hour drive from downtown. Several hotels, including the Grand, have tennis courts and swimming pools. There is a ski lodge at Mt. Hohuan in central Taiwan but the season consists of only January and February.

Boating is available at Green Lake a few minutes from Taipei. Several physical fitness centers have opened in the city. One may also watch Taiwan's Little League baseball team which has won many world championships.

Taipei: Entertainment

Taipei has many nightclubs, such as the Audio City Music Hall, which feature dinner and shows. Prices are reasonable. Check the Hilton, Lai Lai, and Ambassador Hotels for their discos.

British and Australian style pubs are popular. These provide darts, dominoes, and chess games for their patrons. The Waltzing Matilda Inn offers the lowest priced drinks in Taipei during its happy hours.

The Circle, located at the far end of Nanking West Road, should be visited at night. It contains many small food stalls, nightclubs, and theatres. Taipei's West Gate Area, Hsi Men Ting, is the main center for movie theatres, dance halls, and nightclubs.

Taipei: Atmosphere

To enjoy some of Taipei's most interesting sights simply take a walk through some back alleys. At dawn you will find people of all ages practicing the ancient art of Tai Chi Chuan, Chinese shadowboxing. A few old gentlemen still "walk" their birds, slinging a long bamboo pole over a shoulder with a cage at the end. At night strange sounds break the stillness to announce a variety of goods and services for sale by vendors pushing wooden carts. Blind masseurs ask to tell your fortune by playing ancient melodies on flutes. A low rattle indicates the baked potato man is somewhere in the darkness. The noodle man taps his wooden bowl twice. Sleeping people know what these sounds mean and they awake with hunger. Here lives the Old China.

Day Trips from Taipei

One may take many enjoyable day trips from Taipei. At Pitan, Green Lake, which is eight miles south of Taipei, boating is available. At the fishing village of Tamsui some fifteen miles north of the city, one can see Fort Domingo which was built by the Spanish in the seventeenth century. Aborigine dances are the main feature at Wu-lai, which is also near Taipei.

Yang Min-shan, Grass Mountain, is located ten miles north of Taipei. This is a pleasant place with lakes and pagodas which is best visited in the spring to see the flowers blooming or in the fall for the moon festival.

Central Taiwan

Shih Tou-shan, Lion's Head Mountain, located about sixty miles southwest of Taipei, is a Buddhist center. Political dissidents go to its temples for sanctuary and students go there to study for exams. Visitors who have climbed the mountain to visit the temples are met with warm greetings and hot tea. The vegetarian meals are so realistic that "chicken legs" made of bean curd have "veins."

Taichung, located about 120 miles south of Taipei, is the most important city in central Taiwan. From the verdure of fields rich with rice, sugarcane, tea, bananas, and pineapples one can look up at snow-capped mountains. Some fifty miles away is the resort area of Sun-Moon Lake. This lake was once two lakes; both were shaped like their namesakes. They joined when the Japanese built a dam for hydroelectric power and the waters rose. There is an exceptional view from the windows of the Evergreen Hotel.

Taroko Gorge and Hualien are natural wonders worth seeing. The gorge can be reached by flying to Hualien, the only important city on the east coast. Here one can see marble slabs cut into strips. After careful chipping and polishing, objects such as vases emerge from the rocks. Taroko Gorge, "Valley of the Shadows," begins about twenty miles north. The road is cut from solid rock and runs near the bottom of the gorge. This project took ten thousand workers four years to complete. After crossing numerous suspension bridges the road reaches the end of the gorge and Tien Hsiang Lodge, which is small, quiet and serene.

On the slopes of Ali Shan (Mt. Ali) grows a three thousand year old sacred tree. Workers at the reforestry station are busy planting seedlings. Here the Temple of Tsuyin is dedicated to the Goddess of Mercy. Ali Shan is famous for its view of the "sea of clouds" which ring nearby Jade Mountain. When the Japanese annexed Taiwan in 1895, Ali Shan replaced Mount Fuji as the highest mountain in the Japanese Empire and was appropriately renamed "New High Mountain." The railway from Chia-yi was built by the Japanese. It terminates at a station at Ali Shan which is the highest railway station in Asia.

Tainan, 135 miles south of Taipei, was an early trading village. The town was Koxinga's headquarters and a shrine still honors him. Here Chihkan Tower was built on the site of the Dutch Ford Providentia. At An-ping, near Tainan, one may view the remains of the Dutch Fort Zeelandia.

Southern Taiwan

The major port of Taiwan is located at the city of Kaohsiung about two hundred miles south of Taipei. From this port Japanese ships sortied to attack Pearl Harbor in 1941. Here are located the world's second largest drydock and one of the largest oil refineries in Asia. China Steel Corporation is headquartered in Kaohsiung. This industrial center is divided by the River of Love which commemorates the suicide of two lovers by drowning. The river, like the air above it, is polluted beyond belief. Only production and export seem to count.

Tso-ying, a naval base near Kaohsiung, is the major training center for the Chinese Marine Corps.

From Kaohsiung it is not far to the southern end of the island where Kenting Tropical Botanical Gardens exhibit all kinds of floral varieties. Here Kenting House Hotel overlooks the beach. The most southerly town in Taiwan is Oluanpi. On a clear day some people claim they can see the most northern islands of the Philippines from the lighthouse.

Islands

Orchid Island (Lan Yu) is located about fifty miles from Taitung and is accessible by air from Kaohsiung. The island is famous as the home of the White Butterfly Orchid. Yami aborigines sell excellent woodcarvings, flowers, and butterfly displays to tourists. Except for this commercial activity they follow their ancient ways, the men fish and the women farm.

The Pescadores Islands (Penghus) are about fifty miles west of Tainan. They consist of four islands connected by a causeway. The main town of Makung is the center of the local fishing industry. Only the Great Barrier Reef of Australia has more extensive coral reefs than the Penghus.

Quemoy and Matsu are military bastions located almost on the coast of mainland China. Special permission from military authorities is needed to visit these islands.

Things to Learn

Take advantage of the chance to learn something about the world's oldest continuous culture. Many colleges and schools in Taiwan teach Chinese to foreigners. Courses are available in a variety of dialects. Spoken Chinese is easier to learn than most languages and you will enjoy holding basic conversations with local residents.

One can also learn Chinese cooking, calligraphy, Tai Chi Chuan (shadowboxing), painting, palmistry, and herbal medicine. Check the YMCA and newspapers for course offerings.

Activities in the American Community

Taiwan has an active American community. Prominent organizations include the American Legion, the American Chamber of Commerce, Republicans Abroad, Kiwanis, Lions and Rotary. Special interest clubs range from square dancing to Alcoholics Anonymous. At Kaohsiung the American community numbers only 250 people but offers Bible, bridge, and bowling clubs. The Dirty Chopsticks Club meets every second Wednesday of each month and never visits the same restaurant twice.

15. Useful Addresses

U.S. Organizations in Taiwan

American Institute in Taiwan
7, Lane 134, Hsin Yi Rd.
Sec. 3
Taipei
7092000
Ext. 403 for U.S. Passports
Ext. 418 for U.S. Visas

American Information and
Culture Section
54, Nan Hai Road
Taipei
Tel: 3037231

American Trade Center
Asia Enterprise Center
600 Min Chuan East Road
Taipei
Tel: 713-2571

American Chamber of Commerce,
Republic of China
P.O. Box 17-277
Taipei, 10419
Tel: 5512515, 5817089

Taiwan: Chinese Government Agencies

Customs

Inspectorate General
of Customs
85, Hsin-sheng S. Rd., Sec. 1
Taipei

Kaohsiung Customs
3, Je-sing 1st St.
Kaohsiung

Keelung Customs
Harbor Building
8, Kang-hsi St.
Keelung

Taichung Customs
2, Chung Chi Rd., Sect. 3,
Wu Chi
Taichung

Taipei Customs
Chiang Kai-shek International
Airport,
Taoyuan

Trade and Investment Offices

Chinese External Trade
  Development Council
4-7F, 333 Keelung Rd.
Taipei, Sec. 1
Tel: 7382345
Tlx: 21676 CETRA

Joint Industrial Investment
  Service Center
5th Fl., 7 Roosevelt Road,
Sec. 1, Taipei
Tel: 3947217

Investment Commission
8th Fl., 7 Roosevelt Road,
Sec. 1, Taipei
Tel: 3513151

Industrial Development and
Investment Center
10th Fl., 7 Roosevelt Road
Sec. 1, Taipei
Tel: 3947213

Taipei World Trade Center
5, Hsin Yi Road
Taipei, Sec. 5
Tel: 725-111
Tlx: 28094
Mailing Address:
P.O. Box 81-28
Taipei

Special Zones

Export Processing Zone
  Administration, Taipei Office
5th Fl., 27 Paoching Rd.
Taipei
Tel: 3310020

Taichung Export Processing
Zone Administration
Tantze, Taichung
Tel: (045) 224131-5

Kaohsiung Export Processing
Zone Administration,
Kaohsiung,
Tel: 8217141-9

Science-Based Industrial
  Park
Administration
2 Hsin Ann Rd., Hsinchu
Tel: (035) 773311
9th Fl., 201 Tun Hwa N. Rd.

Nantze Export Processing
Zone Administration
Nantze, Kaohsiung
Tel: 3612121-9

Education Relocation, Adjustment (Various locations)

Business Training and
  Development Institute
The American University
3301 New Mexico Ave., #244
Washington, D.C. 20016
(International Executive
Training Course)

Pacific International
  Language School
1451 South King St., #404
Honolulu, Hawaii 96814
Tel: (808) 946-8485
(Mandarin short courses)

Community Service Center
25, Lane 290, Chung Shan N. Rd.,
Sec. 6, Taipei
Tel: 836-8134
(Help with schools, health,
housing, employment,
language, recreation)

VLM Enterprises
P.O. Box 7236
Wilmington, DE 19803
(Relocation: Services &
Publications)

Taiwan: Business Services

Accounting Firms

Andrew Chang & Associates
(Peat, Marwick, Mitchell & Co.)
5 Fl., 742 Ming Shen E. Road
Taipei
Tel: 7138582
Tlx: 23184

Chiang & Lin
(Touche Ross)
13th Fl., 131, Nan King E. Rd.
Sec. 3, Taipei
Tel: 7210211
Tlx: 23757

Chen, Chu & Co.
(Price, Waterhouse)
10th Fl., 142 Chung Hsiao
E. Rd., Sec. 4, Taipei
Tel: 7216686
Tlx: 24241

T.N. Soong & Co.
53 Nan King E. Rd.
Sec. 2, Taipei
Tel: 521-7761
Tlx: 11442

Consulting Firms

China Credit Information
  Service, Ltd.
9 Fl., 30 Kung Yuan Road
Taipei
Tel: 3810720
Tlx: 21034

China Management Consultants
37, Wu Chang St., Sec. 2
Taipei
Tel: 3312862

China Productivity Center
11 Fl., 201 Tun Hwa N. Road
Taipei
Tel: 7137731

Columbia Associates, Ltd.
11 Fl., 96 Chung Hsiao E. Rd.
Sec. 3, Taipei
Tel: 7729731
Tlx: 21808

Kiwi International
  Corporation
(KLB Agencies)
P.O. Box 68-1608
Taipei
Tel: 8711295
Tlx: 28772 DEWIT

International Consulting,
  Ltd.
5 Fl., 66 Min Sheng E. Road
Taipei
Tel: 5414484

Investec (Taiwan) Ltd.
14 Fl., 147 Chien Kuo N. Rd.
Sec. 2, Taipei
Tel: 5316226
Tlx: 28514 Investec

Community Services Center
25, Lane 290, Chung Shan N.
  Road
Section 6, Taipei
Tel: 836-8134

Law Firms

Baker & McKenzie
11 Fl., 205 Tun Hwa N. Rd.
Taipei
Tel: 7126151
Tlx: 21445

Ding & Ding Law Offices
4 Fl., 205 Tun Hwa N. Rd.
Taipei
Tel: 7136300
Tlx: 25077

Huang, Chang & Associates
Suite 302-3, 5405 Chung
Shang
N. Rd., Sec. 3, Taipei
Tel: 5971171
Tlx: 11509

Tracor Law Offices
Floor 11-2, No. 5, Lane 116
Ai-kuo E. Road
Taipei
Tel: 866-2-657-1657

Law Firms (continued)

Kaplan, Russin, Vecchi & Parker
742 Min Sheng E. Rd.
Taipei
Tel: 7128956
Tlx: 23775

Lee & Li
7 Fl., 201 Tun Hwa N. Rd.
Taipei
Tel: 7153300
Tlx: 11651

Tsar & Tsai Law Offices
7A, 25 Jen Ai Road
Sec. 4, Taipei
Tel: 7814111
Tlx: 22732

Other

China Post (English
Language Newspaper)
8, Fu Shun Street
Taipei
Tel: 5943042

Taiwan Stock Exchange
9-1Oth Fl., City Building
85 Yen-ping South Road
Taipei

Overseas Buyers
  Service Center
9th Fl., Union Commercial
Building
137 Nan King E. Rd., Sec. 2
Taipei
Tel: 5515295
Tlx: 283120BSC

U.S. Banks

American Express International
214 Tun Hua N. Road
Taipei
Tel: 7151581

Bank of America
205 Tun Hua N. Road
Taipei
Tel: 7154111

Chase Manhattan, N.A.
72 Nan King E. Road, Sec. 2
Taipei
Tel: 5378100

Chemical Bank
683 Min Sheng E. Rd.
Taipei
Tel: 7121181

Citibank
742 Min Sheng E. Rd.
Taipei
Tel: 7315931

First Interstate Bank
  of California
675 Min Sheng E. Rd.
Taipei
Tel: 7253572

U.S. Banks (continued)

Irving Trust Company
473 Tun Hwa S. Rd.
Taipei
Tel: 7716612

The Morgan Bank
205 Tun Hwa N. Rd.
Taipei
Tel: 7122333

Manufacturers Hanover Trust
62 Tun Hwa N. Rd.
Tel: 7213150

Republic National Bank
205 Tun Hwa N. Rd.
Taipei
Tel: 7182340

Taiwan: Selected Hotels

Taipei

Ambassador Hotel
63 Chung Shan N. Rd., Sec. 2
Tel: (02) 5511111

Asia World Plaza Hotel
100 Tun Hwa North Road
Tel: (02) 7150077

Beverly Plaza
576 Tun Hwa S. Rd.
Tel: (02) 708-2151

China Hotel
14 Kuang Chen Rd.
Tel: (02) 331-9521

Empress Hotel
14 Teh Hwei Street
Tel: (02) 5913261

Grand Hotel
1 Chung Shan N. Rd., Sec. 4
Tel: (02) 5965565

Hilton Taipei
38 Chung Hsiao W. Rd., Sec. 1
Tel: (02) 3115151

Hotel Royal Taipei
37-1 Chung Shan N. Rd., Sec. 2
Tel: (02) 5423266

Imperial Hotel
600 Lin Shen N. Rd.
Tel: (02) 5965111

Lai Lai Sheraton
12 Chung Shan E. Rd., Sec. 1
Tel: (02) 3215511

Mandarin Hotel
166 Tun Hwa N. Rd.
Tel: (02) 7121201

President Hotel
9 Teh Wei Street
Tel: (02) 5951251

Plaza Hotel
68 Sung Chiang Road
Tel: (02) 5515251

The Ritz Hotel
155 Min Chuan E. Road
Tel: (02) 5971234

Taoyvan

Holiday Hotel
269 Dah Shing Rd.
Taoyuan
Tel: (03) 325-4021

Taichung

Formosa Hotel
27 Chung Shah N. Road
Tel: (04) 2226701

Hotel National
257 Taichung Kang Rd.
Sec. 1
Tel: (04) 321-3111

Kaoksiung

Ambassador Hotel
202 Min Sheng 2nd Road
Tel: (07) 2115211

Holiday Garden
279 Liu Ho 2nd Rd.
Tel: (07) 2410121

Taiwan: Selected Restaurants

Cantonese

Canton House
Asiaworld Gourmet
100 Tun Hwa N. Rd.
Taipei   7139966

Cantonese Restaurant
Ambassador Hotel, 2nd Fl.
63 Chung Shan N. Rd., Sec. 2
Taipei   5511111

Dragon Court
Taipei Fortuna Hotel, 2nd Fl.
122 Chung Shan N. Rd., Sec. 2
Taipei   5631111

Ruby
135 Chung Shan N. Rd., Sec. 2
Taipei   5711157

Tiffany's
Hilton International, 2nd Fl.
38 Chung Hsiao W. Rd., Sec. 1
Taipei   3115151

Hunanese

Hunan Restaurant
Hilton International, 3rd Fl.
38 Chung Hsiao W. Rd., Sec. 1
Taipei   3115151

Chinese Restaurant
Ritz Taipei, B1
155 Ming Chuan E. Road,
Taipei   5971234
Peiping

Peiping Palace
Asiaworld Gourmet, 15th Fl. E
337 Nan King E. Rd., Sec. 3.
Taipei 7123114

Shanghai

Shanghai Castle
Asiaworld Gourmet, 14th Fl.
Nan King E. Rd., Sec. 3.
Taipei 7132281

Szechwan

Szechwan Restaurant
Ambassador Hotel, 12th Fl.
63 Chung Shan N. Rd., Sec. 2,
Taipei 5511111

Tze Yuan
100 Nan King E. Road, Sec. 3,
Taipei 5110138

Taiwanese

Joy Leaves
7, Lane 19, Shuang Cheng St.
Taipei 5925555

Mongolian Barbecue

Pepe El Mongol
B, Lane 460, Tun Hwa S. Rd.,
Taipei 7733268

Tien Mou
766 Chung Shan N. Rd., Sec. 6
Taipei 8714677

Western-Continental

Antoine
Lai Lai Sheraton Hotel, 2nd Fl.
12 Chung Hsiao E. Rd., Sec. 1
Taipei 3215511

Europa Haus
21, Chang An E. Rd.
Taipei 5361686

Paris 1930
Ritz Taipei, 2nd Fl.
155 Ming Chuang E. Road
Taipei 5971234

Waltzing Matilda Inn
3, Lane 25, Shuang Cheng St.
Taipei 5943510

Zum Fass
55, Lane 119, Lin Shen N. Rd.
Taipei 5313815

Taiwan: Tobacco and Wine Monopoly

1-1, Nan Chang Rd., Sec. 1.
Taipei 3414505

83, Chung Shan N. Rd., Sec. 2.
Taipei 5410082

362-1, Fu Hsing S. Rd., Sec. 1.
Taichung

16, Pei Men Rd., North Dist.
Tainan

2, Chi Hsien 3rd Road.
Kaoshiung

United States Government Agencies

Agency for International
Development
Washington, D.C. 20523

Department of Agriculture
Foreign Agricultural Service
Washington, D.C. 20250

Department of Commerce
International Trade
Administration
14th Street and Constitution
Ave. NW
Washington, D.C. 20230

Department of Commerce
National Oceanic and
Atmosphere
Administration
National Marine Fisheries
Service
Washington, D.C. 20235

Department of Commerce
Minority Business Development
Agency
14th Street and Constitution Ave., NW
Washington, D.C. 20230

Export-Import Bank of the
United States
811 Vermont Avenue, NW
Washington, D.C. 20571

Office of the United States
Trade Representative
600 17th Street, NW
Washington, D.C. 20501

Overseas Private Investment
Corporation
1129 Twentieth Street, NW
Washington, D.C. 20527

Small Business
Administration
Office of International Trade
1441 L Street, NW
Washington, D.C. 20416

Coordination Councils for
North American Affairs (for Taiwan visas)

4201 Wisconsin Ave., NW
Washington, D.C. 20016
Tel: (202) 895-1800

Suite 1290, 2 Midtown Plaza
1349 W. Peachtree St., NE
Atlanta, GA 30309
Tel: (404) 872-0123

99 Summer St., Ste. 801
Boston, MA 02110
Tel: (617) 737-2050

20 North Clark St., 19th Fl.
Chicago, IL 60602
Tel: (312) 372-1213

2746 Pali Highway
Honolulu, HI 96817
(808) 595-6347

11 Greenway Plaza
Houston, TX 77046
Tel: (713) 626-7445

Penntower Office Center
3100 Broadway, Ste. 1001
Kansas City, MO 64111
Tel: (816) 531-1299

3731 Wilshire Blvd. #700
Los Angeles, CA 90010
Tel: (213) 389-1215

2333 Ponce de Leon Blvd.
Suite 610
Coral Gables, FL 33134
Tel: (305) 443-8917

801 Second Ave., 9th Fl.
New York, NY 10017
Tel: (212) 697-1250

55 Montgomery St., Ste. 501
San Francisco, CA 94111
Tel: (415) 362-7680

24th Fl., Westin Bldg.
2001 6th Ave.
Seattle WA 98121
Tel: (206) 441-4586

16. *Additional Reading*

Archer, Jules. *The Chinese and the Americans.* New York: Hawthorn Books, Inc., 1976.

Chiang Kai-shek. *China's Destiny.* New York: MacMillan, 1947.

Cohen, Jerome. *Taiwan and American Policy.* New York: Praeger Publishers, 1971.

deCrepigny, R. B. C. *China: The Land and Its People.* New York: St. Martin's Press, 1971.

Fei, John C. *Growth with Equity: The Taiwan Case.* Oxford University Press, 1979.

Fraser, John. *The Chinese: Portrait of a People.* New York: Summit Books, 1980.

Geoffroy-Dechaume, Francois. *China Looks at the World.* New York: Pantheon Books, 1967.

Goddard, W. G. *The Makers of Taiwan.* Taipei: China Publishing Company, 1963.

Gordon, Leonard. *Taiwan: Studies in Chinese Local History* New York: Columbia University Press, 1970.

Grousset, René. *The Rise and Splendour of the Chinese Empire.* Berkeley: University of California Press, 1965.

Hofheinz, Roy, Jr., and Calder, Kent E. *The East Asia Edge.* Basic Books, Inc., Publishers, 1982.

Kerr, George H. *Formosa Betrayed.* Boston: Houghton Mifflin, 1965.

Kuo, Shirley W. C. *The Taiwan Success Story: Rapid Growth with Improved Distribution in the Republic of China.* Boulder, Colorado: Westview Press, 1981.

Mendel, Douglas H. *The Politics of Formosa Nationalism.* Berkeley, California: University of California Press, 1970.

Nussbaum, Bruce. *The World After Oil: The Shifting Axis of*

Power and Wealth. New York: Simon and Schuster, 1983.
Riggs, Fred. *Formosa Under Chinese Nationalist Rule.* New York: Octogan Books, 1972.
Scharfstein, Ben-Ami. *The Mind of China.* New York: Basic Books, Inc., 1974.
Selya, Roger Mark. *The Industrialization of Taiwan.* Jerusalem: Jerusalem Academic Press, 1974.
Su, Lung-Yuan. *Foreign Trade Development in Taiwan, Republic of China.* Rohnert Park, California: Sonoma State University, 1983.
Welty, Paul Thomas. *The Asians: Their Heritage and Their Destiny,* 5th ed. Philadelphia: J. B. Lippincott and Company, 1976.
Wilson, Richard W., ed. *Value Change in Chinese Society.* New York: Praeger, 1979.

Periodicals, Brochures, Pamphlets
Asian Wall Street Journal Weekly. 22 Cortland Street, New York, N.Y. 10007
Business Travelers. 82 Fu Shing N. Road, 2nd Fl., Taipei
China Trade and Travel. 12-1, Lane 145, Tun Hwa N. Road, 2nd Fl., Taipei
Doing Business in Taiwan. Price Waterhouse
Investment Guide to Taiwan. Citibank
Taiwan Buyer's Guide. Chinese Productivity Center, P.O. Box 769, Taipei
Taiwan Financial Statistics. Central Bank of China, Taipei
Taiwan Yellow Pages. Available from *China Post,* No. 8, Fu Shun Street, Taipei
Taxation in Taiwan. Deloitte Haskins and Sells
This Month in Taiwan. China Commercial Service, Inc., P.O. Box 68-328, Taipei.
A Republic of China: A Reference Book. International Publications Service, 114 E. 32nd Street, New York, N.Y. 10016

Map Of Taiwan

Tamsui
Chilung
Taipei
Hsinchu
Ilan
Suao
Taichung
Changhua
Hualien
Sun-Moon Lake
Chiai
Sinying
Tainan
Taitung
Kaohsiung

_____ 40 Miles

Index

Global Business Series
from
Jain Publishing Company

Doing Business with Taiwan
ISBN 0-87573-041-8 (paper)
PRICE: $12.95

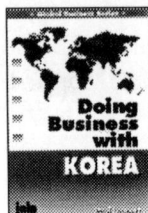

Doing Business with Korea
ISBN 0-87573-043-4 (paper)
PRICE: $12.95

Doing Business with Singapore
ISBN 0-87573-042-6 (paper)
PRICE: $12.95

Doing Business with Thailand
ISBN 0-87573-044-2 (paper)
PRICE: $12.95

Doing Business with China
ISBN 0-87573-045-0 (paper)
PRICE: $12.95

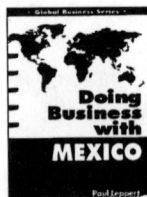

Doing Business with Mexico
ISBN 0-87573-046-9 (paper)
PRICE: $12.95

ORDER FORM

ORDERED BY:

Name _____

Street _____

_____

City/State/Zip _____

Daytime Phone No. (____) _____

QTY	TITLE	PRICE EACH	TOTAL AMOUNT

POSTAGE & HANDLING	Subtotal	
	California residents add 8.25% sales tax	
	Add Postage & Handling	
$3.00 First Book $0.50 Each Add'l.	UPS-Ground add $5.00 additional	
	GRAND TOTAL	

Make check or money order (U.S. dollars) payable to Jain Publishing Company.

[MasterCard] [VISA]   Card No. _____

Exp. Date _____

Signature _____

Ordering by Mail:

Customers using credit cards need only to fold their completed order form in half, tape or staple the free ends and add the correct postage.

Customers paying by check or money order must use an envelope.

Ordering by Phone or Fax:

Credit card customers can order by calling or faxing their filled out order form as follows:

Jain Publishing Company
Tel (510) 659-8272
Fax (510) 659-0501

Please allow up to four weeks from receipt of order for delivery. Thank you!

Cut Along Dotted Line

Fold Along Dotted Line

Place
Stamp
Here

Jain Publishing Company
P.O. Box 3523
Fremont, CA 94539

Attn: Order Department